D0966559

Women in America

FROM COLONIAL TIMES TO THE 20TH CENTURY

Women in America

FROM COLONIAL TIMES TO THE 20TH CENTURY

Advisory Editors
LEON STEIN
ANNETTE K. BAXTER

A Note About This Volume

Johanna Lobsenz directed her skills as an interviewer and writer to disclosing the fate of older women who had to continue working in order to support themselves. Based on scores of interviews conducted in Manhattan, the book analyzes a problem of tremendous emotional impact. In her explorations, which excluded the professions, the author found general agreement among production employers and job agencies that in the late '20s, "older women" meant women after age 35. This is a pioneer study of a kind of double discrimination that persists—discrimination because of age and because of sex. In a review of this book, the *New York Herald Tribune* wrote: "Mrs. Lobsenz has by simply stating the facts of the situation impressed the necessity of improving the status of older women as a matter of fairness and expediency." *The New York Times* stated that she "has made an interesting contribution to what has become a serious economic development and her book ought to stir up discussion of the matter."

THE OLDER WOMAN
IN INDUSTRY

JOHANNA LOBSENZ

ARNO PRESS
A New York Times Company
NEW YORK – 1974

Reprint Edition 1974 by Arno Press Inc.

Reprinted from a copy in
  The University of Illinois Library

WOMEN IN AMERICA
From Colonial Times to the 20th Century
ISBN for complete set: 0-405-06070-X
See last pages of this volume for titles.

Manufactured in the United States of America

———◆———

Library of Congress Cataloging in Publication Data

Lobsenz, Johanna.
    The older woman in industry.

    (Women in America: from colonial times to the 20th
century)
    Reprint of the ed. published by Scribner, New York.
    Bibliography: p.
    1. Women--Employment. I. Title. II. Series.
HD6053.L6 1974   331.3'94   74-3961
ISBN 0-405-06110-2

THE OLDER WOMAN IN INDUSTRY

THE OLDER WOMAN
IN INDUSTRY

BY
JOHANNA LOBSENZ

NEW YORK
CHARLES SCRIBNER'S SONS
1929

TO
MY PARENTS

PREFACE

THE discussion in the following pages does not include the professional woman. The number of years of intensive study necessary for her mastery of any professional field, often extending far beyond her university training, and the added time that must elapse before her work can win recognition, preclude any consideration of age in connection with her work. Moreover, most professional women are outside the necessity of asking others for employment, and, because of this freedom, outside the problems of which this discussion treats.

In this study the term industry has been stretched to embrace not only the types of work usually considered when dealing with women in industry, but also such additional work as women can find in the typical industrial plant, including clerical and general office work, and selling. Domestic work, too, has been included, not only because of its importance per se, but because so many older women can find employment in it.

The term "older" in relation to women in industry is here used to represent a type rather than to mean any particular number of years. It has been found, however, that most employment managers do have a definite age in mind when they speak of the older woman, and that they generally fix it at about thirty-five. Since it is they who decide the age limits at which they will employ new people, that age has been accepted as the starting-point from which to consider her chances for employment.

Because of the extensiveness of the field involved it has been felt advisable to limit this study of the problems confronting the older woman to industrial conditions in Manhattan only. It is aimed to paint a picture of general conditions rather than to make a statistical survey of the fields and chances for employment. The use of figures and tables has by no means been precluded, however, where it was felt that the material could be more vividly presented through their use.

To the many employment managers, placement managers, social workers, and others whom she has interviewed, the author wishes to express her thanks for their uniformly helpful attitude—the expression of their desire to aid in solving the problem under consideration.

In addition, the author owes a particular debt of gratitude to Mr. Willard Huntington Wright. With generous disregard of the many claims on his time, Mr. Wright managed to read the entire manuscript, making corrections with meticulous care, and offering suggestions without which the book in its present form would never have reached completion. For Mr. Wright's endless patience, his kindly encouragement, his unflagging interest, the author is deeply grateful.

If this book can do anything to rouse interest in

the subject, to stimulate discussion of it, to provoke thought about it; if out of it could grow other studies, each taking another phase of the subject, so that a clearer understanding of the older woman's problems, not only by employers, but by the woman herself may result, a step in the solution of her problems will have been taken.

CONTENTS

PART I.   THE PROBLEM PRESENTED

xi

TABLES AND GRAPHS

PART I

THE PROBLEM PRESENTED

CHAPTER I

ITS GENERAL ASPECTS

In the days of Mid-Victorian romance, and before, the number of older women to whom entrance into industry became a personal problem was comparatively small. In addition to the women of the very poor working classes, usually only widows who had been left practically destitute, and spinsters who had no relatives with a home large enough to require their unremunerated services, considered it at all.

The fields to which they aspired were as limited as the number of women entering them. There were small embroidery shops to be kept. There was dressmaking and millinery to do for the neighborhood. There were little inns and little coffee shops to be conducted. And there was always housework to be done for others as a last resort—"taking in washing," if nothing else offered.

Older women who had close male relatives were not expected to go out of their homes into industry. The men of the household, even where their earnings were meagre, would have resented it as a slur on their ability to care for the family. The women accepted resignedly and as a matter of course such provision as was offered. When it was inadequate, it was regarded as a visitation put upon them by a

Father who wished to guard them against too great an absorption in this world's goods.

Where it might have occurred to some older women to enter industry, household duties interfered; for even the simplest old-fashioned home required much personal care. All the women in it could usually find something to do; and at least one woman had to work in it continuously. Cleaning, washing, ironing, cooking, baking, sewing—these things gave even comparatively poor older women a full day's occupation.

But to-day apartment-house life, ready-made clothing and foodstuffs, and modern steam laundries permit many older women considerable leisure. There is not always enough for them to do at home, and many fascinating outside occupations beckon to them.

Thus changing times and conditions have turned from the home into industry this new figure—the middle-aged woman—looming large and ever larger in the business field. With her troop in a new set of industrial problems, bound to grow more and more pressing with the coming years. For she has entered industrial life to stay.

Let us analyze into its component parts the group of women in present-day industry whom we have so far classified by only one common characteristic, that of middle age.

First, there is the typical working woman. Her economic status has always been low. Even after marriage she must face a continuance of gainful occupation outside of the home; or, if she remains unmarried, she must certainly support herself, if not several dependents besides. She is not a newcomer in industry. She has been with us since the days of the first factories, and, even before that, as the hired helper on the farm or in some one else's home. She comprises the group of middle-aged workers who are best known and most numerous, and, therefore, whose problems are the most obvious.

But within the last decade a new group has developed to complicate the situation—a group composed of a number of diverse elements. Its members are usually above stark economic zero. It is, on the whole, the group that used to be content to be shabby-genteel, hiding its poverty. We find in it, first, a considerable number of women whose husbands work but do not earn enough for real comfort. Secondly, there are in it many women who have suddenly been thrown on their own resources. Thirdly, there are the widows who are unwilling to starve gradually on the interest from a bond or a mortgage or an insurance policy. Fourthly, there are the unmarried older women who will no longer assist their married sisters gratis in their household duties. Lastly, there are a few lonely women of some means who refuse longer to be bored. They are of all degrees of skill or the lack of it, possessing a myriad talents, predilections, mutations of background, impulses; and of varying degrees of education. In some cases they have never "worked" before; in others, they are trying to return to work after reverses. Not all of them actually need a job in order to obtain elementary food, clothing, and shelter. But if material comforts raise the standard of living—and few will deny that they do—then these women, reaching out for more of them, are helping to raise that standard; and their efforts to find a place for themselves in industry must be taken seriously. They, too, have been quickened by the modern grope for interesting things, the lure of a fuller life; and they mean to earn the money with which to obtain them.

All these, then, make up the surge of middle-aged women who to-day storm the breastworks of industry. But it is unquestionably becoming more and more difficult for them to go over the top. Both employer and employee admit this, the former sometimes frankly but oftener reluctantly, the latter as a rule vehemently. There are a number of reasons assigned by both sides for this situation, most of which will be analyzed in connection with a discussion of the particular field where they were stated. Some objections, as will be seen, are valid enough from the employer's point of view; only occasionally can one be assigned solely to prejudice against a woman because she is no longer young. Others are not so apparent to the general observer as they no doubt are to those raising the objections.

In some fields, such as selling and factory work, the barriers are gradually but surely being drawn up against middle-aged women in some of the shops, though not, so far, in the majority of them. In secretarial work, typing, bookkeeping, and general office work, the policy of preference for the younger worker has been more or less an unwritten law ever since women entered these industries. Where this policy has been observed, however, it has been exercised much more generally in the hiring of new workers than in the firing of those who have demonstrated their efficiency; although some tendency toward the latter attitude has crept in here and there.

We have, then, as modern industrial factors which we must take into account, first, the army of middle-aged women who want to work, the majority because they must support themselves, the rest because they want economic development; and secondly, the needs and the policies of the various business concerns with whom they must find employment. Granting that the problem is with us to stay, how far are these two factors now in harmony? Where and why do they conflict, and what can be done to bring about a better understanding at both ends? Wherein are the business concerns and their policies at fault, and wherein is the middle-aged woman herself lacking? What are her chances of getting a new position, what her power of holding an old one? What provision has she been able to make against old age, and what has her firm done for her along this line? In what fields, if any, is she more valuable than a younger woman? How can the great body of middle-aged women, older in years and therefore presumably in experience and knowledge of life, best contribute to industry what they have learned, and draw from it in return what they need for further growth and development?

These and many other aspects of the problem press on us for solution. In our attempt to find answers for some of them let us take up the situation as it presents itself in turn to the employer and to the employee. Let us examine some of the principal means chosen by the middle-aged woman to find work, and then some of the most important and most characteristic business fields in which she hopes to find her sphere of effort. We shall limit ourselves to the conditions in that variegated, many-sided centre of commercial activity, Manhattan, New York City, for the way in which the problem in its general aspects presents itself in this industrial centre, is the way it is likely to present itself wherever industry is a leading factor.

CHAPTER II

AS THE WOMAN HERSELF SEES IT

No one realizes more acutely the crisis confronting the middle-aged woman in industry than she herself. Since she is the one whose present position is threatened and whose future is clouded by uncertainty, that is but to be expected.

For a long time appreciation of her position was individual and isolated. Here and there a thoroughly capable and experienced woman, after having given the best years of her life to faithful service in a concern, would find herself suddenly without a position. The death of one of the partners or the process of reorganization was, perhaps, responsible for her plight. Sometimes an ambitious older woman desired to better herself, and, seeing no way ahead in her old place, she was led by confidence in her powers to resign and try for a new post. Occasionally a woman, out of industrial work for many years, sought to capitalize her mercantile knowledge in some emergency. All these women discovered that they shared a common experience. They found that the search for a suitable new position was dishearteningly difficult. Even after they found one, the nature of the work, the surroundings and the salary were rarely what the experienced middle-aged woman regarded as her due after years of approved service. Moreover, she was made aware that the gradually increasing flow of older women into industry was met on the employer's side by a definitely developing policy of preference for the younger worker. These individual women, however, rarely reached any conclusions as to the reasons for the situation.

Gradually the older women fell to discussing the matter seriously among themselves. Then, as more and more of them compared notes, business women's clubs began to hold meetings on the subject. These were in most instances planned rather loosely. Their object was merely to get some general idea of the extent of the problem and to devise some means of combating the evil threatening them. Usually there was no thought of analyzing the situation so as to arrive at a conception of the reasons for its existence.

Superficial though most of them were, they did bring out several interesting angles of the situation other than the views of some of the older women on unemployment. They revealed, for one thing, the types of older women that were having the most difficulty in finding places—so much difficulty, in fact, that they were willing to stand up in a public meeting and tell their stories unreservedly. At the same time, these meetings made it obvious why these women in particular were having trouble, which is a phase of the matter not generally recognized by the older woman herself. They showed, too, that these women created a problem within a problem. For, if the business man's experience had happened to include any of the majority of them, that fact would no doubt color his attitude toward the whole group of older workers.

A brief description of several of these meetings will make these points clear. One of them—probably the first of its kind in the field—was held about two years ago under the auspices of a Business and Professional Women's Club. It came about in this way:

At one of the regular meetings of the organization, one of the members suggested as a possible topic for future discussion the newly developing policy in her own concern. This, the finest department store in Manhattan, where she had been a saleswoman for twenty-five years, had never before shown distaste for older employees; quite the contrary. But now not only were older workers gradually being weeded out, but older people were not being considered for new positions. The reason given was, that these people were too slow in serving customers. And this opinion had found its way into the executive offices via the complaint department. She expressed herself as apprehensive about her own position; wondered what she would do if she lost it, since her salary had never been high enough for much saving; and ended by asking the other members whether they had observed similar tendencies in their own concerns. As it appeared that ten or twelve of them had, it was decided to devote the next meeting to the topic: "Has the Mature Woman a Place in Industry?"

In order to develop the discussion fairly, the employer's side was to be stated by a representative from the personnel office of a prominent Fifth Avenue specialty shop for women and children; while that of the worker was to be presented by a well-known organizer of women into trades-unions. Discussion from the floor was to follow.

The woman from the specialty shop spoke first. She began by denying that there was any policy of discrimination in force in her own organization; declared that her firm had no feeling against the older saleswoman or other worker; and offered in corroboration the fact that they had many such people in their employ. She went on to describe the course of training given their employees for their various duties; and explained that those who profited by it would be retained and promoted. She ended by stating that they tried to put each person where she could work most efficiently, thus giving the mature woman a chance to make her own place.

She was succeeded by the woman from the trades-unions. Herself a middle-aged woman, she declared that women who had started factory work in their early years could rarely look forward to its continuance into middle age, since the nature of the work was such that their strength was exhausted by that time. This not only endangered their present jobs, but often made it practically impossible for them to find work along other lines. She dwelt, too, on the dangers from industrial accidents and occupational diseases; and suggested as counteractions the adoption of the forty-eight hour law, passage of which was then pending, and a possible five-day week.

Here, then, were two widely differing points of view in two totally different industries—naturally a not too logical and a very limited presentation of a many-sided problem. But it was useful because it brought out angles of the whole situation that were more or less general.

The really valuable part of the meeting, however, was still to come. The two hundred women present had listened attentively; and, when the speakers had concluded, they asked questions that were briefly answered and let go again. But it was plain that some of them had something much more concrete on their minds. They wanted to talk about their own experiences; to hear that of others; to find comfort in the knowledge that they were not alone in being thought too old to work well any longer. The questions flickered a bit longer and finally died down. Then the chairman threw the meeting open for general discussion.

One of the first to volunteer her story was employed in a paper factory. Placid, fat and fifty, she smiled cheerily as she described her work, and stated that the only condition made by her firm in keeping their employees was that they do all the work expected of them. They need not fear to grow older; that was but natural.

The next speaker, an aggressive, mannishly dressed

woman, rose in indignant protest. Stout, strident of voice and incisive of manner, she declared that perhaps all was fine in the paper industry; but what about her? Here she was, an expert stenographer; but would any one let her prove it? No. And why? Because she was a little older. No one would even talk to her. The whole thing was an outrage, a shame; and she was tired of it. Abruptly she sat down.

A tall, heavy women of about forty-five, dressed in fairly good taste, then rose. She had held a good position as a social worker; and when this was gone, she had fitted herself for personnel work by courses in a prominent welfare organization. But, so far, neither the organization nor she could find a position where she could fit in. She was soft-voiced, and cultured of manner and of speech; but, after the first five minutes, she left the description of her search for work to express her philosophy of life, which she summed up as "always doing something for somebody."

That sentiment inspired the next speaker, who, after a somewhat clamorous request, was reluctantly recognized by the chairman. Small, neat of figure even though her black costume was a bit superannuated, her mouth set in a perpetual smirk, she recounted her autobiography in a flat, monotonous voice. Since she was twelve years old she had always worked for some one—for her brothers, her neighbors, her friends. After they were all gone or no longer needed her, she tried to find a position where she could work for herself—in what capacity, she did not state. There was nothing for a long time; but finally she found a solution. She became a Christian Scientist; and now, as a healer, could at last do something for others and herself at the same time.

She was followed by her friend, a tall, stately, gray-haired woman, who made a rather good appearance. She was a widow who, at fifty-five, found herself suddenly thrown on her own resources. She had had only a common-school education; had been a home girl, and after her marriage had never been anything but a housewife. No, she did not care for a domestic position; she had kept servants herself. She wanted to work for the Government, and was hoping that some of her political friends would recommend her for a position.

The next speaker was a tall, thin woman of forty-five, shabbily dressed in black. She spoke from the extreme rear of the room; but it took only a moment after she began to turn all heads quickly in her direction. Her voice was beautiful and well modulated; she chose her words tellingly; she could relate the story of her useless search for work movingly. She had been a teacher of stenography, trained in Spanish and French as well as English; she was willing to work as an ordinary clerk now. But no one would give her a chance; she was too old. She was in desperate straits; her room rent unpaid, her meals of the scantiest; her dress spoke for itself. Sympathy welled toward her from the audience; one of those present, a middle-aged women who had opened a real estate office, rose and immediately offered her a position as stenographer, amid much applause. The offer was graciously and gratefully accepted. But the applicant's face, blue-red, blotched, swollen in places, occasioned worry among her hearers. Whether she was very ill at the time, or whether overindulgence in intoxicants had thus registered itself, no one knew. But it was found, on later inquiry, that she had never reported for work; nor could any trace of her be found at the address she had given.

Others there were, too, who spoke, not all of them by any means so hopeless as economic material. The net result on the hearers who were there to listen and to learn, was to send them home heavy-hearted, but with the determination to do everything possible to help them. But what? These women did not want charity. They wanted a chance to be members of the productive element of their community.

Lest this meeting be thought atypical and unrepresentative, it might perhaps be well to describe a few of the women who appeared and spoke at a gathering held in Brooklyn last summer. Its purpose was to weld into a permanent organization the middle-aged of both sexes who had difficulty in finding employment. In this group of several hundred the men outnumbered the women about six to one. A woman, however, volunteered her services as secretary. She was a capable looking, quiet person, fairly modern of dress, who had neatly bobbed her gray hair. She made no comments during the meeting; she merely devoted herself to her duties with all her might.

But some of her sisters were not so reticent. One woman, with blondined bobbed hair and crudely applied rouge, stout and not overneat in appearance, bewailed her lot at not being able to find an office position because she admitted to being thirty-five. As a matter of fact, she looked five or six years younger.

Another woman, tall, thin, and erratically dressed, berated the employment agencies because older women could not get work. "Sometimes they don't even register us," she declared; "and when they do, they just let the applications lie there. They're just grafters; that's all."

A representative of an agency, who was present, answered her. "The agency is just an order taker," he said.

A third woman demanded aggressively why a certain well-known philanthropic organization, instead of helping older women, itself drew age lines. She received no answer. She was not unprepossessing in appearance, but her offensive manner gave some clue to the reason why she was having difficulty in placing herself.

At a later gathering of this same group, one woman blamed the plight of the older seeker for a job on "the blonde that sits in the anteroom and won't let a middle-aged woman get past her to those who do the hiring";—a stricture in which there is unfortunately some truth. But it did not occur to her to think past the blonde to the employer who put her there, nor to wonder why he had done it.

A few more examples of older women and their point of view may be cited. One woman had been private secretary to a department-store head for many years. He retired; and his successor brought his own secretary. White-haired, dignified of bearing, still prepossessing, tactful, smiling and well-dressed in spite of the acutely realized tragedy of her position, she hunted quietly for another job. Months of tireless searching followed the loss of her position. No one, apparently, wanted a white-haired woman. But she kept doggedly on. Finally she did succeed, through a newspaper advertisement, in finding a post as secretary to an editor; and she is still filling it to their mutual satisfaction.

One pitiful woman wrote to the director of the aforementioned Brooklyn club that she had literally begged for a position at twelve dollars a week, so that she could hang on until she summoned enough courage to commit suicide.

Another woman, left a widow at fifty after a comfortable, protected life, tried hard to find employment. For a few months she was cashier in a moving-picture theatre, but finally lost this position because she was considered too slow in making change. Then for a while she addressed envelopes at home. She had a charming apartment, and enough income left to pay the rent for it. She might have let part of her home and covered the rest of her expenses that way, or she might have taken a position in some kind of domestic work, for she was an excellent housekeeper. But she would consider none of these. Her unaccustomed worries finally broke her down. When her effects were examined after her death, she had exactly four dollars left.

An unbridled temper and an inferiority complex that tried maliciously to jab back at an apparently hostile world, were another woman's chief instruments of her own undoing. Slim and of medium height, careful to keep her dark, simple clothing presentable, she was blessed, too, with a fresh complexion and fairly good features. Unfortunately, though, her mouth, a trifle tight, was well pulled down at the corners, and her eyes, large and handsome, had in them a restles light. But in spite of these things, because she looked capable and energetic she usually succeeded in getting the routine positions for which she applied. It was hardly a week or two afterward, however, before she "resigned," and was on the hunt for another post.

"I wouldn't let them tell me what to do," was her favorite explanation, usually given with a toss of the head. "They think they're more than I am. But I tell 'em. Those foreigners can't give an American orders."

The case now to be cited was chosen because the would-be employer began with absolutely no feeling of prejudice against the hiring of an older woman.

The applicant had inserted an advertisement for work as a substitute stenographer. She described herself as an expert. Summoned to a law office in answer, she proved to be middle-aged, somewhat erratic in dress, nervous and excited of manner. She listened as her would-be employer outlined her duties.

"What do you pay?" she demanded.

"Twenty-five dollars a week," was the reply.

"What!" she shot at him. "You have a nerve! I advertised that I was an expert. How dare you expect that kind of service at such a price?"

"I'm sorry," the lawyer answered, "but that's what the position pays."

The woman rose and flounced out. Shortly thereafter she was back.

"Do you mind if I use your phone?" she inquired.

"No, go right ahead," he replied.

She called the number of the office from which she was then telephoning.

"Why, that's my number," remarked the surprised lawyer.

"Well," she said, "I'll tell you. In an office down the hall there I talked up to the man and he called the porter to put me out. I ran back here for safety."

The lawyer went out into the hall. There, indeed, was the porter.

"Did a lady get into your office?" he asked the lawyer.

"That's all right," was the reply. "Just let her alone. There's nothing the matter."

He waited until the porter had disappeared, and then turned toward the applicant.

"The man's gone," he said. "I think you may go now." And she departed, leaving the lawyer to a consideration of the undesirability of employing older women.

Most of the cases discussed reveal the older woman in her more unfortunate aspects. Some of these women do not realize the importance of a neat personal appearance as a business asset. Some show lack of ability to concentrate for any length of time along a given line of thought. Some display minds that not only do not work logically but hardly function at all. Others, much worse than that, have become warped, bitter, narrow in mental outlook. A few have let their less desirable traits so dominate them that they have become almost unemployable.

Because these things are so, it may be argued that in her more unfortunate aspects. Some of these woman seeking employment. That may be quite true. It will be recalled that these were only a few of several hundred women present, all of whom had, or were threatened with unemployment problems. The vast majority may easily have had none of these idiosyncrasies. In order to understand better how they do fit in, we shall regroup the middle-aged women seeking work outside of the home, this time on the basis of their preparation for commercial life.

There are, first, the two general groups of the skilled and the unskilled workers. Those who are skilled may again be subdivided into two classes; the highly specialized group, and the routine workers.

In the highly specialized group, the spectre of unemployment in middle age rarely stalks; for the woman in it has made herself a master in some field where her services are usually in constant demand. She may be a milliner who can design her own hats; a dressmaker who can create her own models; or a housewife who has evolved a new kind of bread or cake or jam. Or she may be a secretary who, not content with the mastery of the mere technic of stenography and typing, has, in addition, increased her fund of information not only generally, but specifically in the field where she is employed. Or she may be a saleswoman who has learned, besides the routine information about her stock, something of its origin, its manufacture, and its possibilities.

Along with her intensive technical equipment, the highly skilled worker in any field has usually cultivated the gentle art of getting on with her fellow-workers. Besides, the consciousness of hard work thoroughly done in trying to master her field, has given her a wholesome feeling of self-respect. She reflects this in her carriage, in the care of her person, in the manner of her dress. She has an "air." Business men and women recognize it, and feel confidence in her. She may advance in years, but she can never grow old in the sense of dropping out of touch with new movements in thought and with better industrial methods. She does not lose her enthusiasm, for she understands her work; and this gives her a solid foundation on the basis of which she is always ready to try new methods. Her passing years but add to her experience, and her interpretation of each new experience increases her value. She is alert mentally, poised emotionally, well physically. She is no problem.

It is largely in the ranks of the routine workers and the unskilled workers that difficulties arise at the approach of middle age. Work of this kind includes the clerical positions, such as elementary bookkeeping, stenography, typing, and filing, and the use of the modern counting machines. The average selling positions, factory work, and some of the simpler phases of the various trades, such as the elementary processes of hand sewing, may also be included.

This type of work was not, as a rule, very hard to master. In consequence, not only did many of their contemporaries find it as easy of access as they themselves did, but the younger people of a similar type coming into industry found it just as simple. The result was that the field became overcrowded faster than business expansion could absorb the constant influx of new workers. In the resultant competition for the available places the middle-aged workers were sometimes worsted.

Usually these were the less competent ones or, for some other reason, the less desirable workers. Buffeted by misfortune as these women frequently were, many of them had developed a defensive attitude. They resented their condition, and yet were unaware of how it had come about, for they were not equipped to analyze their own troubles. And now that they had grown older, they regarded that fact as another piece of hard luck, which the world held against them, though it was no fault of their own.

Most of the cases that we have cited, where they were not totally inexperienced commercially, came from this poorer section of the routine group. They discovered what looms as a danger to all routine workers as they grow older—namely: the fact that because routine work is so easy to acquire and so easy to duplicate, they are the first to suffer from changes in mercantile policy based on age groups. The bent of mind displayed by the women we have discussed may be merely superficial. They may sense only vaguely the currents of commercial policy underlying their condition. But such perceptions as they have are rooted in truth, and to that extent are shared by the far larger group of routine workers of which they are a part.

There is unquestionably a growing prejudice against employing older women, and, what is more, a marked tendency evincing itself in some quarters to eliminate those already employed. Older women come into contact with this attitude on the part of employers when, in their search for new positions, they find the bars put up sometimes at thirty, sometimes at thirty-five years. They are hurt and puzzled, and also apprehensive about the whole situation. They cannot account for it. They feel that they are able to work, and that they have many more years of usefulness left in them. What has happened?

Perhaps the great body of older women who come up against the newer order of things may never have met the less desirable types we have discussed here. It may be that, far from being crochety or ill-kempt, they are cheerful and neat. They have worked hard all their lives. They have become good, serviceable, average bookkeepers, or clerks, or office workers, or salespeople. If they have been with a firm for many years, they are apt to feel themselves, perhaps too strongly, an indispensable part of it. If they are try-ing to get into a new concern, they are likely to feel pride in the years of experience they can offer their prospective employer. They are dazed by the new order of things. Feeling for the company of others in like case, they hold meetings to discuss the situation. They listen as the more unfortunate among them tell their stories; and the various hearers are stirred in various ways.

Some may wonder vaguely how these women, going about as representatives of the older women in industry, affect the whole question of the middle-aged woman's chance of getting work. They may feel that business men, if they were to meet only these, might judge the whole group unfairly. Others among them are likely to sympathize with them in their troubles, and to consider that denying them a chance can hardly rehabilitate them. They may let their minds follow a little along the road their unfortunate sisters have described. They may understand that these women were perhaps the most poorly equipped of them all to take it. They, perhaps still in possession of a job, may let their imaginations follow a bit further. Suppose that they and twenty or thirty other women like themselves that they knew should lose their jobs. They, too, would have to go through the grind in search of a new place. They would have to tour the agencies, answer newspaper advertisements, call at employment offices. They would meet the usual deprecatory smile, the disheartening "I'm sorry—nothing to-day," not only to-day, but for weeks and months thereafter. How long would they be able to retain their confidence in themselves? How much of it could they take before they, too, would become bitter? How long before they would acquire that sense of uselessness, that loss of spirit, which follows one's being made to feel that one has become too "old" to be needed any longer? Would any of them, breaking under the strain, become like some of the cases about which they had just heard?

Still others of the listeners may try to find reasons for the older women's situation, and thus discover the blonde who keeps them out in the passage, the married women who hold on to their jobs instead of doing their housework at home, the young people crowding them out of their places, and the employment agencies who will not send them out in answer to calls. Here and there a rare spirit may ask: "What other reasons, besides age, can there possibly be for the fact that I can't find work?"

But to most of the older women the situation is an ominous one. It may be surprising to some that they do not analyze it a little more keenly, both from the standpoint of industry and from that of their own shortcomings, until it is remembered that analyses are most successfully made from a vantage point of repose and security. That moment in which a rock is about to crash down on one's head is not likely to be the one chosen for a consideration of the causes back of its loosening from the mass.

CHAPTER III

"HELP WANTED" AND "SITUATIONS WANTED"

I

THE middle-aged woman who is trying to find work has three principal channels open to her. They are, first, the classified "want" columns of the newspapers; secondly, the employment agencies; and lastly, the personnel managers of the various shops and industrial units.

She will usually begin her search by answering advertisements. Should this procedure alone prove unsuccessful, she will generally supplement it by inserting an advertisement herself, setting forth her qualifications.

If she cannot find a post through the newspapers, her next step will probably be to register with the employment agencies that specialize in her type of work. In most cases she follows up her registration by daily visits to the agencies, in the hope that a call for her may be put in while she waits.

But rarely does the call come; and, disappointed, she next goes the rounds from office to shop, from one employment manager to another, hoping that somehow she will succeed in finding a position. Sometimes she does; but oftener she discovers that managers usually advertise for new people when they require them. So finally she goes back to the news-papers.

Advertisements, then, are the first means resorted to by the older woman in her attempts to find work; and on the whole they remain her favorite medium. There are a number of reasons why this is so. To be-gin with, they appear to her to offer a much larger number of positions and a much wider range of oc-cupations than do the employment agencies. More-over, she knows through these notices that a cer-tain number of positions are definitely available; and the compensation for each is, as a rule, clearly mentioned. Then, there are no expenses to be in-curred beyond the purchase of a newspaper, or the cost of the insertion if she herself advertises. Besides, and more important than anything else perhaps, she may present herself directly to the firm offering the position, thereby eliminating the preliminary weed-ing-out process that is exercised by the placement clerk in an employment agency. And, finally, there are no fees to be paid if she succeeds in obtaining a position.

So she picks up the paper eagerly. The hope that springs eternal in all human breasts takes an extra leap in hers; for there are almost two full pages of advertisements calling for workers. Surely where there are so many gaps in the industrial world wait-ing to be filled, there will be ample room for her.

Let us assume that she is trying to find a place as

a domestic worker. She scans the three or four columns headed "Household Help Wanted—Female." The chambermaids must all be young; but since there are no age qualifications mentioned in the majority of the advertisements calling for cooks, she carefully checks the most promising of these, and reads on. There are a number of calls for housekeepers; but too many are like the following:

"Housekeeper for furnished room house; room and $20 monthly."

The positions for houseworkers are better. Most of them ask for girls or young women; but some make no specifications as to age; and these she checks also. There are a few advertisements that call definitely for middle-aged women. One follows:

"Woman, elderly; Catholic can have good home for a few hours' housework."

There is no mention of compensation. She recalls several others of a similar trend which she had clipped and kept because she thought that there must have been some mistake. She takes them out, lines them up on the table, and reads:

"Woman, elderly, to offer housekeeping services, return room and board with elderly man and invalid wife."
"Woman, middle-aged; assist with housework; good home and $10 monthly."
"Woman, elderly; charge country house; furnace; $10 monthly."

She counts the advertisements in the issue before her that offer household positions to middle-aged women. Out of a total of 173 notices, there are just seven; and of these seven two are of the type mentioned.

She may be a clerical worker instead of a "household help." Does she fare any better? In the issue just examined there are thirty-three calls for bookkeepers, eleven for clerks and comptometer operators, twenty for typists, and twenty-five for stenographers, exclusive of the advertisements inserted by agencies. Of these, making a total of eighty-nine, not one of them asks definitely for a middle-aged woman; on the contrary, many of them read like these:

"Bookkeeper, under 30 years, Christian preferred; at least 3 years' experience; full charge books; salary start, $25."

"Bookkeeper, young lady, with high school education, commercial course; must have some experience typing, posting and bookkeeping; Gentile."

"Clerk, Christian; permanent position, with advancement; state age, salary desired, and previous experience, if any."

"Stenographer; Christian; state age, experience, and salary."

One interests her for a moment.

"Typist; home copying; bobbed heads not wanted."

But as she does not own a typewriting machine and suddenly has an unaccountable desire to bob her hair, she finds it necessary to let this opportunity go by. She gets ready instead to investigate such clerical positions as do not make some stricture or other as to age or religion. Out of eighty-nine calls, there are thirty that offer her a possible chance of employment. So she sets out to visit those among them that may be answered in person, leaving the rest for later attention in the event of her unsuccessful return.

Sometimes the woman reading the "Help Wanted" notices belongs to neither of the two classes mentioned. She may be a new entrant in industry, who has been forced into the field by untoward circumstances. What chances has she of finding work?

She discovers at the end of the advertising columns offering positions a number of engaging invitations, apparently framed for just such as she.

"Women," reads one, spread over a full quarter of a column,

"An Organization
Controlling
Several Banks
With Present
Deposits Totalling
Over $22,000,000

With a program for future expansion that is gigantic in scope

Headed By
Prominent Bankers
Is Offering You
A Permanent Connection

with immediate earning possibilities, on a commission basis so enormous that, not wishing to be doubted, we

don't care to mention figures, and what possibilities for
advancement
TRULY AMAZING
We want every woman reading this ad. regardless of
experience or the kind of work she has been doing, whether
employed or unemployed, to attend one of our Securities
Sales Meetings scheduled for

Monday, 11 A.M. & 3 P.M.
Tuesday, 11 A.M. & 3 P.M.
No one will be admitted
After the scheduled hours."

Realizing at one and the same moment that the
days of the ballyhoo were not quite over and that
the enormous commissions to be earned from the
sales of "securities" were probably as secure as the
stock she would have to handle, she reads on:

"Women," says another, "(Christian) (Protestant)
earn extra money. Only 50 days to Xmas. No experience
necessary. Pleasant, profitable day or evening work, especially adaptable for housewives, teachers, active church
workers, clerks and salesladies; highly cultural work;
call from 9 A.M. to 7 P.M."

And further down the column still another:

"Women—Are you tired of the commonplace? Do you
want a steady, interesting position? We pay you a salary
of $5 day to start. You must be past 28 years, honest and
sincere; experience unnecessary as we give you free
training. Call Monday 9–12."

And again:

"Women—How would you like to sell a health work
without the usual resistance of 'I can't afford' 'must con-

sult my husband,' etc.? These excuses are eliminated because our work is moderately priced; experienced women
earning huge sums in salaries, bonuses, and extra commissions. See or write Mr. *** "

Wondering what was left for the publishers of a
moderately priced work after the huge sums in "salaries, bonuses, and extra commissions" were paid to
their agents, but suddenly recollecting that she is
hunting a job, she turns at last from this column to
the one frankly labelled "Canvassers."

Is the newspaper advertisement, then, as good a
medium for placing the middle-aged woman as she
commonly thinks it is? In order to come to some conclusion on the subject, let us examine the "Help
Wanted" and the "Situations Wanted" columns in
the Sunday editions of two newspapers, the New
York *Times* and the New York *World,* for the five
months from July to November, inclusive, of the
year 1927. This particular period was chosen because it covers the seasonal fluctuations in industry,
from the dull summer months, over the period of
normal fall activity, through the preparations for
the Christmas rush. The decision to use these two
newspapers was based on the fact that, since each
reaches its own large segment of readers and of advertisers, taken together they would give a fairer
picture of employment conditions than if either were
to be considered alone.

In examining the twenty-two Sunday issues of
each of these newspapers some general observations
come first to our attention. For instance, *The World*

has 22,090 positions offered and 7,475 sought. *The Times* reverses this situation. It shows a total of only 9,436 positions available, as contrasted with 12,559 advertisers looking for work. Then again, the types of work offered in each newspaper differ somewhat. There are advertised in *The World,* for example, a total of 1,550 positions in bonnaz, finishing, dressmaking, lampshade making, crochet beading, and similar work. In *The Times,* there appear only seventy-one calls of this kind. On the other hand, thirty-seven buyers are offered positions through *The Times,* but only thirteen through *The World.* Fifteen saleswomen try to find places through the former, but only four through the latter.

Apparently, then, each of these newspapers has points of preference over the other in the minds of those offering or looking for work. The middle-aged woman, too, shares this feeling. If, for example, she is a houseworker who desires to find a place through *The Times,* she will advertise her qualifications herself rather than consult the newspaper's announcements of positions open. The fact that she does so is shown in the totals for this type of work over the period under consideration. There are only seventy-eight requests for middle-aged houseworkers in that time, but 233 older women inserted advertisements. If she prefers *The World,* however, she is as apt to wait for her prospective employer to advertise as she is to put in her own notice. This fact is shown in the totals: 181 notices for help and 207 for positions.

If she is an experienced clerical worker, she is

much more likely to advertise her qualifications in *The Times* than in *The World;* for there are fifty-six applications from her in the former and only seventeen in the latter. But, on the other hand, she is offered forty-four positions in *The World* as against only thirty-three in *The Times*.

On the employer's side, too, these preferences are perceptible. There are 937 calls for saleswomen in *The World,* and a little less than half that number, 455, in *The Times;* and 900 insertions for canvassers in *The World* as contrasted with 769 in *The Times*. Of the miscellaneous positions, which cover such occupations as advertising workers, forewomen, managers, and store detectives, *The World* offers 160 and *The Times* 104.

The following graph summarizes the positions both offered and sought in each newspaper, showing the proportion of older to all women in each case:

FIGURE I
PROPORTION OF MIDDLE-AGED TO ALL WORKERS
July–Nov., 1927

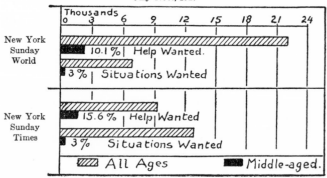

So far, only the general features of these "Want" advertisements have been considered. In order to evaluate more fully the place of these notices as aids in finding work for the older woman, the "Help Wanted" and the "Situations Wanted" groups must each be analyzed separately.

II

Let us examine first the offers of work appearing in *The Sunday Times* for the five months we are considering.

Referring to Table I, the total number of "Help Wanted" advertisements for all the occupations listed is 9,436. Of these, 1,476, or 15.6 per cent, are either definitely open to middle-aged women or else give no age restriction. There are included, among others, 769 positions for canvassers, 455 for saleswomen, thirty-seven for buyers, and 104 for miscellaneous occupations. Of these, the advertisements for canvassers usually call specifically for an older person.

But explanation is necessary regarding the selling, buying, and miscellaneous groups. Since these notices do not definitely call for the middle-aged woman, they, including the miscellaneous positions, must be regarded as offering a chance of employment to older women rather than a promise. Care has been taken to exclude from the tabulation all advertisements that call for young women, and to enter only

FIGURE II. TABLE I

POSITIONS OPEN TO MIDDLE-AGED WOMEN AND TOTAL POSITIONS OPEN TO ALL WOMEN

Data from Advertisements in the New York *Sunday Times*, July-Nov., 1927

Issues	Household	Clerical	Buyers	Selling	Canvassers	Misc.	Total Middle-aged	Total All Ages
July 3	3	1	0	15	5	3	27	198
10	1	1	2	11	31	6	52	444
17	2	1	0	1	8	3	15	318
24	0	2	0	16	28	3	49	384
31	7	0	0	1	28	8	44	350
Aug. 7	3	1	1	19	29	9	62	374
14	1	5	1	20	26	6	59	390
21	3	4	3	22	32	1	65	397
28	2	3	4	36	25	6	76	480
Sept. 4	4	1	4	25	16	9	59	310
11	10	5	0	42	32	9	98	707
18	8	1	8	35	48	10	110	580
25	8	1	2	33	45	6	95	554
Oct. 2	3	0	2	24	47	3	79	571
9	3	0	2	36	43	1	85	533
16	1	0	2	19	49	6	77	516
23	5	4	0	18	44	4	75	434
30	3	0	1	15	49	4	72	437
Nov. 6	6	2	1	17	46	2	74	365
13	1	0	0	13	55	0	69	371
20	2	1	4	16	42	3	68	370
27	2	0	0	21	41	2	66	353
22	78	33	37	455	769	104	1,476	9,436

those where thorough experience was required, or where the wording otherwise indicates that a middle-aged person would be considered eligible. Due weight is given to the fact, for instance, that salesmanship is one of the few fields still remaining where experience and capability are held to be more important than the question of age. Then, too, the advertisements for salespeople inserted by the large department stores rarely call for only one person. As a rule, the number of applicants required varies anywhere from two to one hundred. This fact may be regarded as neutralizing any overweight that may have been given to the middle-aged woman's chances in selling.

Buyers have been included because it is reasoned that the work of buying, to be carried on successfully, requires many years of training. This being so, the women engaged in it are automatically carried into the middle-aged group.

Notwithstanding these things, it must be conceded that the older woman is only a probable, not a certain, factor in filling these positions. Therefore, if we deduct their number, a total of 596, from the 1,476 possible chances for older women, we have left 880, or 9.3 per cent of the whole number of positions. In other words, we find that through this medium the older woman may find 15.6 per cent of all the work offered, including miscellaneous occupations, possible of attainment. But in only 9.3 per cent of it is she sure to be the first choice.

Turning to Table II, we discover first that there are

FIGURE III. TABLE II
POSITIONS OPEN TO MIDDLE-AGED WOMEN AND TOTAL POSITIONS OPEN TO ALL WOMEN

Data from Advertisements in the New York *Sunday World*, July–Nov., 1927

Issues	Household	Clerical	Buyers	Selling	Canvassers	Misc.	Total Middle-aged	Total All Ages
July 3	5	1	0	8	16	3	33	364
10	3	3	0	20	39	10	75	759
17	2	1	1	23	38	13	78	747
24	9	1	0	21	39	10	80	705
31	7	0	1	20	21	3	52	779
Aug. 7	3	1	0	31	22	3	61	934
14	7	0	1	49	25	9	91	989
21	7	2	0	37	26	11	83	1,053
28	13	1	1	50	18	5	87	1,124
Sept. 4	10	5	3	41	21	6	86	760
11	7	4	0	94	41	33	179	1,795
18	12	5	0	8	35	6	66	1,500
25	6	3	1	61	41	19	131	1,137
Oct. 2	13	0	1	57	53	2	126	1,217
9	13	5	0	59	58	4	139	1,342
16	16	3	0	67	62	5	153	1,240
23	10	3	0	51	42	3	109	1,102
30	8	0	0	34	74	3	119	1,028
Nov. 6	8	0	0	41	61	5	115	965
13	4	4	3	66	53	4	134	905
20	8	2	1	49	59	3	122	870
27	10	0	0	50	56	0	116	775
22	181	44	13	937	900	160	2,235	22,090

many more positions offered in *The World* than in our first medium. The total here is 22,090, more than double that of *The Times*. As may be seen from a comparison of the two tables, each occupation listed shares in this gain except that of buyer. Are the chances of the middle-aged woman for obtaining work increased because here positions are so much more numerous?

The total number of calls in *The Sunday World* possible of attainment to the older woman, computed on the basis used in working with Table I, is 2,235, or 10.1 per cent of all the positions advertised. Again deducting the groups not definitely asking for middle-aged workers, for which the total is 1,110, the number of older women specifically called for is 1,125, or 5.1 per cent, which is a little more than half of what it was in *The Times*. The increased opportunities created by this gain in places offered, then, are all for the younger workers.

One set of advertisements has been omitted from Table II, even though there appear in them no specific age limits. This is composed of calls for dressmakers, embroiderers, bonnaz workers and crochet beaders, finishers, and similar work in the sewing trades. In all there are 1,550 of these notices. Although young workers are not usually called for in them, inquiry at the headquarters of the two chief national unions covering these trades revealed the fact that most of the workers in them are young. The most famous woman organizer among them puts their average age at twenty-five years.

The majority of the exceptions to this are employed in factories and small shops that "give work out." Here payment is, as a rule, made on a piecework basis. The employer has therefore little reason to be concerned with the age of his workers. Lack of speed on their part can react unfavorably only on themselves; so undoubtedly the middle-aged woman who knows these trades can find work under this system. But nothing in these advertisements is definite enough to establish sound bases for a computation of their approximate number. It was therefore thought better to omit them entirely from the tabulation.

Table III, which gives the combined figures for the "Want" advertisements of

FIGURE IV.   TABLE III

TOTAL "WANT" ADVERTISEMENTS, JULY–NOV., INCLUSIVE, 1927

	Help Wanted		Situations Wanted	
	Middle-aged	All Ages	Middle-aged	All Ages
New York *Sunday Times*..	1,476	9,436	375	12,559
New York *Sunday World*..	2,235	22,090	235	7,475
Totals...............	3,711	31,526	610	20,034

Total Percentage of Middle-aged Women, Wanted, All Occupations...11.7
Total Percentage of Middle-aged Women, Advertising, All Occupations...3.0

both newspapers, shows a total of 31,526 positions offered to all women, out of which number 3,711 present a chance of employment to older workers.

Are all these 3,711 opportunities of actual economic value to them? That is doubtful. For too often the positions to which they may aspire offer little of a definite or permanent nature. This is obvious in advertisements like the following, which are not included in the tabulations:

"Woman wanted, young or middle-aged, who has a small bald patch on her scalp; wanted for demonstration of new hair insertion treatment. No compensation. For further particulars call *** "

But many of the canvassing positions as well are of dubious value as a definite source of income. And canvassing includes a large segment of the positions an older woman is asked to fill.

The following is a typical example:

"Solicitor—High caliber woman wanted to solicit pupils for large legitimate music school where all instruments of modern orchestra are taught; liberal commission basis."

Here is another:

"Saleswoman—Satisfy the desire down deep in your heart to get away from your present unprofitable field. You've promised it to yourself many times.
Make note of this 'phone number now.
Call between 10–12 A.M. for appointment.
If under 35, we cannot use you."

And this:

"Lady, socially well connected with the upper class of New York, can materially increase her income by serving as a means of bringing a high ethical dentist's name before her socially prominent friends; liberal compensation on a percentage basis. Phone Monday, Columbus *** "

This one is more decent, but offers little to hold to as a means of support:

"REAL ESTATE SALESWOMAN

Mature woman of education and refinement, preferably experienced, can earn large income selling our Lake *** Club property; generous commission, thorough cooperation, and legitimate, live leads."

One is led to wonder what ancient grudge the following advertiser was trying to settle:

"Ladies, refined, and school-teachers, for pleasant outside work, selling real estate; salary and bonus."

Here, indeed, is an inspiring call:

"Women: Curiosity leads you to answer many advertisements; a real desire, provided you are sincerely seeking a profitable connection, will lead you to answer this one; no capital, no experience, no special ability needed; start now.—Call all week, 9–12."

These advertisements for canvassers, under various guises, make up a total of 1,669 out of the 3,711 positions open to older women in both these newspapers together for twenty-two Sunday issues, or five months of their heaviest circulating editions. After we deduct these from the 2,005 advertisements we have before listed as asking directly for middle-aged women, there remain only a few household and clerical positions, a bare 336 out of 31,526 places offered, in which she has a reasonably sure chance of supporting herself.

III

Some of the older women prefer to insert their own advertisements. What is the ratio of these to the women who would rather answer them, as shown by a comparison of the figures for "Situations Wanted" with those for "Help Wanted"?

By consulting Tables IV and V, we find that the total number of older women seeking positions through *The Sunday Times* in all the occupations is 375. In *The World* it is 235. This gives us a total of 610 middle-aged women who took this means of finding work, out of a total of 20,034 women of all ages who tried for positions in this way. In examining these figures more closely, we see that in *The World* only twenty-eight of these are for other than household positions. In *The Times* the number exclusive of domestic work is 142. In both these newspapers, then, the household workers do the bulk of the advertising for positions, *The Times* carrying a slightly larger number than *The World,* 233 to 207. But the

FIGURE V. TABLE IV

SITUATIONS WANTED; MIDDLE-AGED AND ALL OTHER WOMEN

New York *Sunday Times*, July–Nov., 1927

Issues	Household	Clerical	Buyers	Selling	Canvassers	Misc.	Total Middle-aged	Total All Ages
July 3	2	0	0	0	0	3	5	219
10	5	1	0	0	0	2	8	435
17	4	0	0	0	0	0	4	340
24	4	0	0	0	0	2	6	343
31	3	4	0	0	0	0	7	282
Aug. 7	7	13	0	0	0	4	24	309
14	3	4	0	1	0	2	10	295
21	8	3	0	1	1	3	16	329
28	5	1	0	0	0	3	9	381
Sept. 4	5	7	0	0	0	0	12	284
11	26	3	0	4	0	13	46	733
18	17	1	0	0	0	7	25	734
25	21	1	0	2	0	1	25	756
Oct. 2	10	2	0	0	0	1	13	828
9	11	3	0	0	0	1	15	844
16	13	2	0	1	0	0	16	904
23	20	5	0	1	0	5	31	912
30	18	1	0	0	0	8	27	737
Nov. 6	18	1	1	2	0	6	28	817
13	6	0	1	3	0	5	15	754
20	14	3	0	0	0	2	19	694
27	13	1	0	0	0	0	14	629
22	233	56	2	15	1	68	375	12,559

FIGURE VI. TABLE V

SITUATIONS WANTED; MIDDLE–AGED AND ALL OTHER WOMEN

New York *Sunday World*, July–Nov., 1927

Issues	Household	Clerical	Buyers	Selling	Canvassers	Misc.	Total Middle-aged	Total All Ages
July 3	2	0	0	0	0	0	2	175
10	3	0	0	0	0	1	4	356
17	5	0	0	0	0	0	5	252
24	3	0	0	0	0	0	3	210
31	1	0	0	0	0	0	1	259
Aug. 7	5	0	0	0	0	0	5	237
14	7	1	0	1	0	0	9	194
21	2	2	0	0	0	1	5	200
28	5	1	0	0	0	0	6	228
Sept. 4	8	0	0	0	0	0	8	175
11	7	0	0	0	0	1	8	408
18	17	1	0	0	0	0	18	437
25	25	2	0	0	0	0	27	440
Oct. 2	13	3	0	0	0	2	18	443
9	10	2	0	1	0	0	13	398
16	15	0	0	1	0	0	16	502
23	18	0	0	1	1	0	20	472
30	6	0	0	0	0	0	6	431
Nov. 6	18	0	0	0	0	0	18	415
13	17	2	0	0	0	0	19	467
20	11	1	0	0	0	0	12	408
27	9	2	0	0	0	1	12	368
22	207	17	0	4	1	6	235	7,475

former is apparently much more highly regarded than the latter as a medium for obtaining work in the other fields. This is indicated by the 142 notices covering them in *The Times* as compared with the twenty-eight in *The World*. This ratio remains true to the tendency shown by women of all ages in this regard; for, as has been previously pointed out, *The Times* carries nearly 5,000 more "Situations Wanted" advertisements over the period we are considering than does *The World*.

It will be noticed that in this tabulation of situations wanted a total of ninety-three advertisements appears in both newspapers together for such positions as salesmanship and miscellaneous work. But they may not be deducted from the total of 610, as was the case with the "Help Wanted" groups. That is because, even where the maturity of the advertiser is not definitely stated, these notices are so worded as to leave no doubt in the mind of the reader concerning the age period of the applicant. Subtracting, however, two advertisements inserted by canvassers, we may compare the 608 notices remaining with the 336 positions offering older women fairly continuous employment. We find that the ratio of older women advertising for secure positions as against such positions calling for older women is approximately two to one.

This ratio of two to one may mean that the older woman finds advertising for work more efficacious than answering calls. On the other hand, it may indicate a desperate last effort to be placed on the part of older women who have failed to acquire a position by answering advertisements. No doubt both premises are true to some extent. Domestic workers who advertise in *The Times,* for instance, expect their prospective employers to read their applications rather than to call for them through "Help Wanted" announcements. This is indicated by the fact that there are in this medium three times as many "Household Situations Wanted" notices as there are "Help Wanted" calls.

But the fifty-six applications in *The Times* for clerical positions support our second premise. The fact that older women usually do have difficulty in finding work in this field gives added weight to this reason for the comparatively large number of these notices. The sixty-eight applicants for miscellaneous positions in *The Times* and the six for these various occupations in *The World* both point in this same direction.

In tabulating the notices of "Situations Wanted," the many advertisements of dressmakers looking for employment were omitted. According to the figures given in the Fourteenth United States Census, 22,-758 dressmakers in Greater New York work outside of factories. Of these, a total of 6,562 are forty-five years of age or older. There is also an additional 11,-693 between the ages of twenty-five and forty-four. Taking one-half of this number, in order to approximate the group between thirty-five and forty-four, and adding it to those we know are older than that, we have a total of 12,409 dressmakers, or 54 per cent, who may be considered middle-aged.

But they are not trying to find a place with any one concern. Their work operates very much like that of an independent *entrepreneur*. They may easily make clothes for seventy-five or eighty different customers in the course of a single year. If efficient they gradually build up a permanent clientele, as does any shopkeeper. They do not, therefore, fit strictly into the situation we are considering in connection with the middle-aged woman at this point; but we shall have occasion to refer to them again later on.

Lest it be thought that the older seeker after work has all the difficulty on her side, a few of the insertions among the "Situations Wanted" may here be quoted.

Quite unconscious of the fact that it might be fair to offer her prospective employer some guarantee of experience, one woman's notice reads:

"Woman, mature years, seeks position cashier, saleswoman, anything not menial."

An employer considering the following applicant might have some difficulty in fitting her into the narrow confines of one business:

"Intelligent, all around business and professional woman wants executive position with reliable concern; travel preferred. Miss *** "

In order to meet the requirements of the following advertiser murder may be necessary:

"Housekeeper, German-American; middle-aged; motherless home preferred; $100."

This applicant's list of qualifications has evidently strayed into the "Situations Wanted" group out of the "Personal" column:

"Housekeeper, refined, middle-aged, fine cook, sewer, piano player, charge widowers' home; wages $75."

Advertisements like the last two are all too common among those labelled "Household Situations Wanted—Female." If there are as many motherless homes as there are women looking for positions in them, something must be causing super-mortality in this particular group. Some of these middle-aged seekers for household work are willing to admit wives, but draw the line at children or at more than two people of any age in the family. Many show preference for business people who will leave them unsupervised in the home all day. Others will work only in small apartments. Some ask for all these things together.

If the shortage among domestic workers is so acute that these middle-aged applicants are in a position thus to set their own terms, why do not more older women try this sparsely cultivated field? Is the objection to doing "anything menial" so deep-rooted?

It is hard to understand the grounds for its existence. One need only glance over the "Household Situations Wanted" columns either in the issues quoted or in any other newspaper. One is apt to come away with the conviction that if there be a menial in the transaction, it is not the prospective employee.

IV

Do the ratios obtained in this study of newspaper advertisements offer any support to the contention, so often made, that middle-aged women must often face discrimination against them in industry?

It has been found in the foregoing pages that an average total of only 12.8 per cent of all the positions advertised in two newspapers over five months might possibly be filled by middle-aged women; and that an average of only 7.2 per cent of them were certain so to be filled. But these ratios are not necessarily of themselves evidences of discrimination. If they are much lower than is to be expected from the proportion of all middle-aged working women in Greater New York to the total of women of all ages employed there, then there may be some ground for the formulation of a conclusion. It may then be considered that at present fewer older women are being admitted into industry than formerly, despite the increasing number trying to enter it.

By referring to Table VI, we find that in Greater New York, out of a total of 609,344 women of all

FIGURE VII. TABLE VI

NUMBER OF WOMEN IN SELECTED OCCUPATIONS
IN GREATER NEW YORK, ARRANGED BY AGE
PERIODS

Data from the Fourteenth United States Census, 1920

Occupations	All Ages	25–44	45–64	65 or Over
Manufacturing...	204,129	75,706	21,302	1,782
Transportation...	23,010	5,874	582	31
Saleswomen.....	27,278	12,433	2,662	86
Clerks..........	12,191	3,593	575	16
Packers.........	1,471	381	128	7
Domestic.......	156,667	84,916	42,291	4,654
Clerical........	184,598	51,535	5,005	198
Totals........	609,344	234,438	72,545	6,774

All Occupations, Total 45–65+.... 79,319
½ Total 25–44...... 117,219
———
Total Middle-aged............ 196,538
Total % Middle-aged, Greater New York............32

ages in the occupations we have considered, 79,319
are over forty-five years old. But there is a group
of 234,438 women between the ages of twenty-five
and forty-four years, some of whom must obviously
also be middle-aged. One-half of these have here
been taken as the approximate number above thirty-
five years old, which brings the group of middle-aged
women workers in Greater New York to 196,538, or
thirty-two per cent of all women employed there.

Table VII gives the Federal Census figures for
Manhattan Borough only. Since the newspapers here
considered are Manhattan publications and adver-

FIGURE VIII.   TABLE VII

NUMBER OF WOMEN IN SELECTED OCCUPATIONS
IN MANHATTAN, NEW YORK CITY

Data from the Fourteenth United States Census, 1920

Occupations	All Ages	25–44	45–64	65 or Over
Manufacturing...	99,722	39,526	11,089	874
Transportation...	8,475	2,424	213	12
Saleswomen.....	12,722	6,255	1,235	39
Clerks..........	5,425	1,680	264	5
Packers.........	742	180	72	4
Domestics.......	106,330	60,463	26,877	2,572
Clerical.........	66,254	20,971	2,334	109
Totals........	299,670	131,499	42,084	3,615

All Occupations, Total 45–65+.... 45,699
½ Total 25–44...... 65,749

Total Middle-aged............111,448
Total % Middle-aged, Manhattan............ 37

tise primarily the requirements of its particular readers, these figures are perhaps of more weight in this
connection than the totals of Table VI. But the percentage found here does not differ very widely from
that obtained for all New York City. Here it is thirty-seven per cent, as against the thirty-two per cent
found for all the boroughs together.

For the occupations considered in our advertisements, these ratios are almost three times as high as
the twelve-per-cent average that was found to include the positions possible to older women in two
newspapers together over a period of five months.

It is easy to infer from a comparison of these ra-

tios that older women are finding it three times as
hard now to obtain places as it was seven years before, when the census figures were compiled. But
may we not more safely conclude that these newspaper advertisements represent only the floating
group, the turnover, of middle-aged women? May
we not assume that the total of all older women together, including those who still hold positions as
well as this twelve per cent that is trying to find
them, will be at least the thirty-seven per cent it
was before? To all of which must be added the further modifying circumstance that some older women
are constantly finding employment through the two
other means we have previously mentioned—direct
resort to employment managers, and registration
with employment agencies.

V

Whether the particular percentages quoted are
admitted or not as evidence of discrimination against
older workers, the advertising columns themselves
leave no room for doubt that it exists. The following
notices demonstrate, first, that middle-aged women
are being definitely barred from applying for work
with certain firms; and secondly, that some concerns
so manage their employment offices that no older
woman who has not grown up with the firm can ever
enter it.

"Saleswomen—" reads one—the same firm, curiously enough, whose personnel manager had declared so forcibly only two years before that it followed no policy of discrimination against older women:

" *** & Co. require well-appearing young saleswomen with high grade retail experience for full and part time positions in the following departments:

> Millinery
> Jewelry
> Sportswear
> Hosiery
> Neckwear and Flowers
> Misses Coats and Dresses
> Women's Coats and Dresses."

This firm, it will be observed, has put up the bars not only for the millinery, coat, and dress departments, where older women are usually preferred, but also for the part time positions. These latter are for the most part sought by older women who must fulfil home duties for part of the day.

Another firm—the same department store whose policy had been observed with so much apprehension by one of its older saleswomen two years before—inserted the following for several consecutive weeks:

"SALESWOMEN

" *** & Co. require several young women of intelligence and good address, thoroughly qualified to sell in the following departments:

> Leather Goods
> Corsets
> Toilet Articles

Domestics
China and Glassware
Gloves."

Here again several departments formerly considered the prerogatives of older saleswomen have been closed to them. In this case they are the corset, domestics, and china-and-glassware sections.

In this instance, night work, too, is denied them:

"Young Women up to 35 Years of Age
$18 per Week
and advancement in salary assured.
Night Telephone Operating."

The following advertisement clearly indicates that older women are definitely excluded from seeking new positions with this concern:

"Clerks
Young Ladies
17–25 Years of Age
No Business Experience necessary.
Hours 9 A.M. to 5 P.M.
Splendid Opportunity for Advancement
All Higher Positions Are Filled by Promotion."

One large chain tea room has the following:

"Cooks: age 20–35; assistant cooks, short orders, vegetable cooks, carvers, steam table servers; permanent, good pay; advancement to those who qualify; hours 12 noon–9 P.M."

The same firm also inserted this:

"Woman, white; age 20–35, scrub 7 A.M.–4 P.M. also 8–5 P.M. $18, lunch."

A third call for help issued by this same firm reads:

"Ushers—Age 20–30 years, 5 feet 6 inches or over. Hours 12 noon–3 P.M. Apply Monday."

This last advertisement appeared in the above form for three consecutive weeks, and for three weeks before that with the word "tall" instead of the more precise "5 feet 6 inches" of the other notice. The other two advertisements also appeared for several weeks each. Evidently the number of young women who were willing to begin scrubbing at seven A.M., or to surrender each evening until nine P.M. cooking vegetables and guarding steam tables, or who had the happy combination of youth and a height of five feet six inches, were not easy to find.

One more advertisement may be quoted before we leave the subject. This was inserted by a well-known chain restaurant corporation:

"Waitresses. The *** Restaurant Company desires a limited number of intelligent English-speaking young ladies, ages 18–25, preferably with some experience in waiting on tables; permanent positions, good pay; best of working conditions. Apply between 9–11 A.M."

These all form tangible evidence that older women are actually being denied employment in some places.

What, on the whole, is the value of the newspaper advertisement as a help to the older woman in finding work? It has been stated that 7.2 per cent of the

"Help Wanted" notices call certainly for older women, and that 12.8 per cent do so tentatively. It has also been noted that 610 out of 20,034 applications for work, or three per cent, are requests from older women. In spite of these small percentages newspaper advertising is, for the present, one of the most important aids the older woman has in obtaining a place.

CHAPTER IV

THE EMPLOYMENT MANAGER AND THE
PROBLEM

I

As a rule workers, middle-aged women included, have more or less consciously in mind their own idea of what constitutes a good position. When they apply for work they automatically compare what is offered with this mental picture of what they would like to have. Rarely do the two coincide.

Few applicants understand that a very similar process is going on in the mind of the personnel manager who interviews them. He, too, compares subconsciously those who come to him with his conception of the employees he wishes to obtain. Experience with thousands of applicants has developed in him a set of reactions to various types which serves him as a basis for classifying his first impressions. He has these reactions and the information on the application blank to guide him. Thus armed, he chooses from the group available to him those who clash least with his conception, and trusts that a minimum of maladjustment will result.

He does this, of course, within the bounds laid down for him by the general policy of the concern which he serves. Some concerns may give him more leeway than others; but seldom has he an absolutely free hand in carrying on his work. The general procedure that he is to follow is, as a rule, determined by the Board of Directors of his firm. He attends the conferences where these policies are outlined; and he may volunteer suggestions as to the operation of his department. But in the last analysis his work must articulate with that of the rest of the organization.

He may be in charge of employment in one of those numerous corporations formed in recent years by the merging of smaller individual concerns. Whatever his personal views on the hiring of older women may be, in such organizations his procedure is fairly well outlined for him.

The single firms that to-day form these merged groups appreciated, in the days of their independence, the part that their experienced employees had played in building up the business. They pointed with pride to workers who had grown up with the firm, had served it twenty, thirty, forty years. They paid bonuses to the employees after a certain definite term of service. But they are single firms no longer. Their trade names may still appear on products made by the merged concern; for these names had long ago won the public confidence, and are still of distinct commercial value. But their individual entities are gone; and with them usually their consideration for their old employees.

Sometimes the more valuable of the older workers are retained by the merged group. But since one reason for the merger was to reduce operating expenses and thus declare larger dividends, the value of any item that tends to raise these expenses beyond absolutely unavoidable limits is questioned. Such items are higher salaries and higher group insurance rates for older workers. So the employment manager receives his instructions for the hiring of new workers, which do not usually include provisions for employing older women.

In some fields, however, the employment manager is a freer agent. The nature of the business which he serves demands that he be allowed to judge for himself to a large extent the desirability of any applicant. Such a field is that of selling.

Since the saleswoman is the direct point of contact between the store and the customer, she is, for the moment, virtually the firm itself. Therefore her personality is of first importance. Fortunate indeed is the shop whose employment manager recognizes this, and lets no consideration of age or salary modify his determination to get the best possible saleswomen for it.

II

Selling and clerking in stores, according to the Fourteenth Federal Census figures, engages the time of 5,510 middle-aged women in Manhattan Borough alone. This comparatively large number seems in itself evidence of a lack of discrimination against older women in this field at least. And to some extent this is true.

In order to get representative data concerning selling, the nine largest department stores and the five largest and finest specialty shops for women in Manhattan were visited and their employment managers interviewed.

Of the nine department stores, all but one of the personnel managers were men. Of those in the five specialty shops, four employment offices were also managed by men. This leaves two large-scale shops out of fourteen whose employment managers were women—which is particularly interesting in view of the fact that these two were the very shops whose advertisements requesting young women were quoted.

In six out of the remaining twelve, women assisted the employment manager. They gave out, read, and sorted applications, and did the preliminary interviewing and eliminating. In the other six shops, men exclusively attended to the hiring and firing of the women employees. Would it be better for the older woman were there a woman at the head of all fourteen of these offices?

Of the six that had women as assistants, three declared themselves as opposed in general to the hiring of middle-aged women employees, for reasons which will be noted later. A fourth was willing to hire them if they were capable and efficient. How she could judge of that without trying them out she did not explain. The remaining two were, on the other hand, strongly in favor of hiring them. Of the six where the employment managers were exclusively men, exactly the opposite situation prevailed. Four of these declared themselves decidedly in favor of older women. The other two, for varying reasons, were quite as much disinclined to hire them. Summarizing this situation, we find that out of these fourteen large shops six, as a general policy, preferred older women; seven did not; and one had no objection to them if they were capable and efficient.

Of the six that did prefer them, four were men. Does this fact warrant us in assuming that men are more inclined to hire older women than are members of their own sex?

Two points lend color to this assumption. First, the two offices that drew the line most rigidly at the employment of older women were those managed entirely by women. Secondly, the only two offices with women assistants that favored them were those in which very young women frankly echoed the policies of their male chief. Of the remaining four, one, as has already been stated, would not keep out a capable older woman. The other three would not hire them if they could avoid it. But whether the last three were acting on their own initiative or following the policies of the men at the head of their offices, cannot be stated. Assuming, however, the latter to be the case, these three men, plus the two who were definitely opposed, make a total of five men against hiring them. But three with women assistants and four without, a total of seven, will engage them. Thus both our questions are answered at once.

III

In gathering the data relative to the feeling of employment managers about hiring older women, personal interviews were chosen in preference to the mailing of formal questionnaires. But in order to understand just what set of conditions were more or less general in the selling field as far as the older woman was concerned, these questions, among others, were uniformly asked in each office:

1. Do many older women apply here for work?
2. Are their applications welcome, or would you rather not engage them?
3. Are older women without previous experience ever given employment? If so, in what capacities?
4. When older women are hired, do they make good? In what departments are they better than others?
5. Are they absent from duty more than are younger workers on account of illness and home duties?
6. What percentage of your total sales force is made up of older women?
7. When they grow too old to work well in their own fields, are they transferred to other jobs? Is there a pension system for them?

It was found that all fourteen shops continually had older women applying for work. The average proportion of these was ten per cent of all those who sought for positions. Most of these were salespeople. A few asked for work in sewing and alterations; some wanted to be matrons or packers; but these last called, as a rule, only in response to advertisements for such help. There were also some applications from older clerical workers.

As to the preferences of these shops regarding older women, it has already been pointed out that six of them welcomed such applicants. These were chiefly the specialty shops. Out of the five visited, only one admitted a preference for younger workers—the specialty office in charge of a woman manager. Herself middle-aged, but slim, nervous, active, bobbed-haired, and preserving a general air of youthfulness, she declared that her shop had no set policy against older workers. It employed them chiefly in the infants' wear departments and in the alteration rooms. It had, too, some elderly saleswomen in its employ who had been with the firm for many years. But it did not care to hire new older women if younger people could be obtained instead. Her chief objection to middle-aged women was that she found them set in their ways and less adaptable than younger women. She felt that it was unfortunate if some older women had found it hard to get new positions; but considered that it was "up to the women to get the training that would prevent this."

In the other four specialty shops an entirely difference situation prevailed. In two of them, fifty per cent of the saleswomen were middle-aged. The total sales force amounted to 850 in one and 500 in the other. In the third, ten per cent of the force of 750 were older women; and in the fourth, thirty-three per cent out of 450 saleswomen. In these four shops together, there were approximately 900 older saleswomen to be found, or an average of 35.3 per cent of all their saleswomen combined.

Older women found opportunities in these partic-ular shops, according to their employment managers, just because these establishments were specialty shops. The public patronized them because it ex-pected of them expert knowledge of its requirements in their field. It did not expect such knowledge to be characteristic of beginners or of young workers generally. Therefore the older woman who knew her work thoroughly was an asset to these shops, and they were glad to employ her. One manager declared that the most efficient salesperson of their entire force was a woman well advanced in middle age.

All these four shops stressed the necessity of a de-sirable personality on the part of the older woman they would employ. Two of the managers tried to define it. One emphasized the avoidance of make-up, and a generally neat, dignified appearance. The other laid particular weight on a gracious manner, and on the courtesy that springs from good home background strengthened by a real desire to be of service. He did not consider that a young person pos-sessed sufficient knowledge of life to have developed these qualities fully.

He pointed out too that the older woman usually possessed superior knowledge of her work, owing to her longer experience. He felt that all these qualities combined made older women more desirable than younger in the work of selling in a first-rank specialty shop. He explained that a really valuable employee in any business must be a "finished product," and that it took time and experience to produce that result. He showed that all the higher positions in the shop, such as buying, were filled by older women.

One of the two department stores that favored the employment of older women did so for much the same reasons. This, a first-rank shop whose trade consists largely of conservative older people, freely employs older women in all its departments except those occupying the main floor. The reason they are not put there is because on that floor are displayed the little luxuries that women buy—the trinkets, flowers, laces, scarves, ribbons, and novelties of all kinds. Younger women are considered better for selling these. But in the other departments older women are thought more desirable. A tour of the shop showed that they were also employed about the building in various types of repair work, and as matrons.

The other department store, a more popular but fairly good shop, also hired older women freely. But here the employment manager apparently did so more because he was disgusted with the younger generation than because he found superior qualities in older women. He called the older saleswomen members of the "old school," and insisted that they worked better and harder than young people. He felt that they were more responsible. He declared that they knew their "three R's," for one thing, and their business, for another. They were more satisfied with conditions, more resigned, more afraid to change. He did not particularly laud these last traits as qualities; he felt that staying too long in one place, for instance, put one in a rut. But as characteristics in his sales force he was quite charmed by them.

In all these shops older women are sometimes engaged even if they have not had any previous business experience. They are put on the general-sales force and at first, as a rule, are given charge of special tables. If they prove that they can sell, they are then transferred to places behind the counter. Women who do not ask to sell are placed at packing, in the alteration rooms, and as matrons.

The older women who are employed in these six shops, then, find their work more or less appreciated. Their positions are fairly secure as long as they continue to exercise the qualities for which these employment managers chose them.

But in some of the other shops they are not held to be so desirable. The assistant manager of one department store, a young man comparatively new in the personnel field, was quite bitter against them. He said frankly that if he had his way he would "throw them all out to-morrow." He mentioned as one of their faults the fact that they had lost their enthusiasm. He declared that they did not work well; that they were cranky and indifferent; hard to get along with. He divided the group of older workers into two classes; those between thirty-five and forty-five, and those older. The latter he called "absolutely impossible." No, he did not have the power to discharge those already in the shop, many of whom had served the firm for years. But no more older women were to be taken on, except for certain departments, such as the house furnishings, where young people did not care to work. They were too lacking in adaptability and too unpleasant to deal with.

Of 2,000 saleswomen in this shop, twenty-five per cent were older women. If this young man continues to be assistant manager there for any length of time, apparently 500 more older women will have an excellent chance of getting out of their "rut" to find new positions.

One firm, with a normal sales force of 3,000 that rose to 4,500 during the pre-Christmas sales, took on as few older women as it possibly could. According to its assistant manager, the chief reason for this was because they wished to keep such readjustment positions as they had for their own workers as they grew older. New selling positions were filled by young people. Here, too, the older woman was considered too hard to manage and too conservative. Forty per cent of their saleswomen were, however, more than thirty-five years old; which suggests a recent change either in store policy or in employment managers, or both.

Another manager of a department store in which women exclusively hire the women employees, echoed the usual complaint about the inadaptability of the older woman. But she stated that the real reason why they were not being hired wherever avoidable was because of the pension system. That was so in spite of the fact that length of previous service did not necessarily presuppose the retention of employees until they reached the pensioning age. All employees understood that theirs was but a day to day contract, terminable whenever the exigencies of store policy demanded. This last is entirely at variance with the procedure in this shop before the death of its founder several years ago. In all this great shop this manager could not find a single department where older women could render more valuable service than their younger sisters.

In one department store which employs 2,500 saleswomen, the assistant manager weeded out ninety-five per cent of the applicants before the employment manager interviewed the rest for hiring. Neither she nor the manager objected to older women as such, and engaged them occasionally if they were very capable and experienced. But rarely would they hire an older woman in any capacity who had never before been employed. This assistant felt that older women would not care to work for the salaries willingly accepted by beginners or slightly experienced girls. Then, too, no one who was not herself advanced in years liked to give an older woman orders.

The manager of another shop declared that it was not the policy of his firm to refuse to hire older women, or to try to weed out old employees who had given years of service to this long-established department store. But in every case where a vacancy was to be filled, he preferred younger workers. He disclaimed any personal responsibility for this preference, and laid that at the door of the public, which, he declared, wanted young people to serve them. The growing feeling in some quarters against older women he called a social condition, which the employment manager simply took as he found it. Older women were not startled or surprised by it, he said. They expected to reach the time when their desirability was ended. Business, he remarked, was run for efficiency; and those workers were hired who were most efficient. No, he did not think that older women were less adaptable; on the contrary, years of selling experience made any one adaptable. But younger people had more "snap."

One assistant manager attributed the adverse attitude of her firm toward older women to the fact that her firm was "building for its future," and young employees could serve them longer. They tried to keep their old employees as long as good health remained. But they did not like to hire new older women because of the pension.

In the minds of department-store and specialty-shop managers, then, older women were adaptable or conservative, gracious or "cranky," able or incompetent, according to the individual manager's point of view and somewhat also according to the types of older women who had come within the circle of his experience. But whether they worked well in some places because they knew they were wanted, or were wanted because they worked well, it is hard to say. Probably the two were correlative.

Many of the employment managers agreed that older women, when hired, as well as those already in their employ, most decidedly made good. They were preferred in most shops in the millinery, coat, dress, fur, infants' wear, house furnishing, upholstery, dress goods, and furniture departments. Most managers found them regular in attendance, even in cases where they also had home duties.

Not many shops provided graduated positions into which to shift their employees as they grew too old to do their regular work efficiently. Only two—both department stores—mentioned having such a system. But questions as to its operation failed to bring very definite replies. It is difficult to see how an effective method along these lines could be developed, if only for the reason that most older women would resent being deposed from their positions and shunted to less important ones. The realization that they were considered too old to be any longer useful in their field would probably hurt more than any resultant reduction in salary. Most shops, rather than attempt such readjustment, have devised instead for their aging workers some form of pension.

Only two of the fourteen shops here considered admitted that they made no provision whatever for women workers who grew too old to serve. As the manager of one put it, older women were not discharged because of their age provided they could keep on their feet and do the work. Beyond that, apparently, no further thought was taken for them. Both this shop and the other that made no pension provision for older women, were among those that hired them unrestrictedly.

In two of the remaining twelve, pensions were granted after twenty-five years of service; in seven others, after thirty-five years. In the other three they were sometimes granted in individual cases, but not as a regular practice. In none of the shops was pensioning automatic. Cases were usually reviewed by officials of the concern, and each decided on its merits. In none of these shops did the employees contribute to a pension fund, though they did to a welfare fund which gave them a weekly allowance for a specified time in case of illness.

Higher group insurance rates to protect the employer were no doubt influential with some employment managers as a reason why older women were not considered desirable workers in their shops. These rates range from forty-seven cents a month for workers of sixteen to $2.52 a month for those of sixty. For workers of thirty-five, the rate is fifty-eight cents a month; for those of forty-five, eighty-six cents. In addition there is non-occupational disability coverage for its women workers as a whole, regardless of age. This ranges from a minimum of $.083 a month for firms whose women workers number eleven per cent to a minimum of $.163 for concerns where the women workers number ninety-one to one hundred per cent.

In reviewing the procedure of these various employment offices, one realizes how much they reflect not only the general policies of their firms, but also the personality of the managers themselves. That, of course, is inevitable in any work. But in their case the point of view they hold is not alone important for the concern with which they are affiliated. It is of even more importance for the thousands of women whose livelihood depends on their decisions.

IV

What are the older woman's chances of finding work in factories? That depends a great deal on what the factory is making.

In order to arrive at some conception of the situation in this field, six factories, each representative of a different industry, were chosen for investigation. These were: the largest plant for the making of fountain pens in New York City; a nationally known cracker and cake bakery; a fashion pattern making plant, also nationally known; a dress factory; a candy manufacturing plant formerly known throughout the country, but now only a unit in a huge merged group; and a gigantic plant for the making of electrical supplies.

The employment manager of the fountain pen making plant expressed himself as quite willing to hire older women at any time. They were especially desirable in the repair department, and for the work of cleaning pens. There were better positions in the factory for them too; all the heads of departments were older women. If they were clerical workers he could, in particular, find work for them in filing. Nor was this all. He pointed out that a tour of his firm's extensive retail shops would reveal the fact that nearly all their saleswomen were middle-aged.

He explained why he so patently preferred them. He found them more steady and less "flighty" than the younger workers. He felt that they put into their work the energy spent by the younger group on the pleasures natural to their age. He was convinced that the concern got more out of their work; that they "paid."

The work in this factory was such that there was no severe physical strain at any point. A great deal of it had to be done by hand; and such machinery as there was, was small and of delicate construction. The older woman, therefore, had no great need of agility of movement, though undoubtedly she had to be dexterous and careful in her work. Besides, the machines that were used were not dangerous. In view of these things, it is easily comprehensible that older women could be employed in large numbers in this plant.

A somewhat similar situation prevailed in the pattern-making factory. The plant is part of a unit which in its entirety comprises a well-known fashion magazine publishing company. This part of the enterprise employed the services of approximately 800 women; of these, twenty-five per cent were middle-aged.

Older women were often engaged here without previous experience. Since the work they did was easily learned, such lack was not serious. They sorted and folded the millions of tissue paper patterns that formed the stock in trade of this particular factory. As their work was paid for largely by the piece, if they were slow the loss was theirs rather than the concern's. Here, again, there was no dangerous machinery to handle. The only thing that might possibly have proved an undue strain was the fact that they had to stand practically continuously in order to do the work rapidly. They did not, however, appear to mind that. The skilled piece workers earned from twenty to thirty dollars a week; those who preferred a time wage received fifteen. The work was somewhat seasonal.

The employment manager here, too, preferred older women because he found them steady and reliable. He attributed these qualities to the better training that, in his opinion, they had received in the schools of yesterday. He employed young girls as clerical workers, because the factory office required only elementary knowledge. Highly skilled, expensive work was wasted there. The forewomen were, for the most part, older women who had been promoted from the ranks.

In neither of these factories was there a definite pension system. However, meritorious cases were considered and some provision made for them. In the pattern factory this took the form of a sick benefit payable up to a period of three months, even though the worker may have been in its employ for a comparatively short time. After that, the worker was allowed to "drop out."

The older woman has more difficulty with dress factories, according to the employment manager of one of them, who was a woman. She pointed out that operating was too great a physical strain on the average middle-aged woman. About ten per cent of their employees were older women, some of whom had been with the firm for many years. These workers did basting and finishing, as a rule.

An even less favorable situation prevailed in the cracker factory. Here the employment manager, although expressing the utmost sympathy with the older woman's attempts to get work, admitted that he himself hired very few of them. He rarely engaged workers above forty-five, or, for that matter, at any age approaching it. He explained that the nature of the work was such that an older woman could not do it. The machines were too difficult and too dangerous to handle for one not in her first youth. The movements required in managing them were too rapid for the middle-aged.

The total average force of this factory was 3,500 women. The few older workers on its payroll had been with it for years. They worked in the locker and rest rooms, caring for them and keeping them neat; some mended the girls' uniforms.

In this factory there was a pension board that reviewed meritorious cases. A favorable decision resulted in half pay.

This employment manager seemed to feel that the pressure of home duties, especially on the married workers, made older women less fit for factory work. This was especially true of the worker who had no grown daughters to lend a hand after the entire family returned in the evening from its labors. A middle-aged woman could not be expected to stand very long the double strain of running a household and working in a factory where speed was necessary. So, although the higher group insurance rates did have a share in determining his adverse attitude, the chief reason why this manager preferred not to hire older women, was, he stated, because he thought they could not stand the inevitable strain.

The manager of the candy making plant explained that the year before, when the firm had been merged with several others, their entire force of 1,500 women had been transferred to the factory of another concern in the group. Of these shifted workers, ten per cent were older women, many of whom had been with the original concern for years.

In their present plan of organization they had little need for the services of older women, but hired them occasionally as matrons. The managers of some of their many retail shops scattered throughout the city were older women who had come up out of the ranks of their salespeople. But they were not engaging new workers of the older type.

This manager found that the older women who were still with them were regular in attendance and reliable in their work. Such difficulty as he had with them on rare occasions he attributed to the fact that they were as a rule taking care of homes as well as working in the factory. This concern had no pension system at the time, but was attempting to work one out.

Two questions asked by this employment manager threw some light on his attitude toward the hiring of older women. He had explained that the firm had entered a merged group. Then he inquired:

"Have you noticed any change in our stores lately? Don't you think they look brighter, fresher, now?"

Apparently he felt that the conservatism that had heretofore distinguished this particular concern had been a liability. Perhaps he thought that a lack of middle-aged women would help among other things to eliminate this condition.

The electrical plant employed a force of 12,000 women in all its various departments. In spite of this large number, middle-aged women had little opportunity to find work in it. For, as a general rule, no woman over thirty years of age was even engaged. This rule operated with particular stringency in the field of relatively unskilled labor and with regard to the clerical force.

This concern found that young people were much more efficient than older for their special kind of work. There were some older women on their payroll, however. Thirteen per cent of their total woman power was over thirty years old; and two-tenths of one per cent was over fifty. These older women were for the most part to be found in the supervisory and executive positions. In this concern there was a graduated system of salary increases that kept pace with years of service to a definite maximum; and a pension system that began to operate at fifty years after twenty years of service.

Summing up the situation regarding the employment of older women in these six factories, two preferred older women and four did not. The two that hired them did work that required little speed or concentration. Moreover, where machinery was used it was easily managed and not dangerous. A system of piece-work payment obtained rapidity where that was thought necessary.

In three of the other four, speed was a prime requisite and the machinery was heavier and more dan-

gerous. In the candy factory and in the electrical
concern the chief obstacles to the employment of
middle-aged women seemed to be those generally incident to the hiring of such workers in large-scale
merged groups.

It may occasion surprise that older women do not
find factory work especially plentiful in the sewing
trades. A walk through the garment centre during
any lunch hour will reveal two facts. First, the proportion of women in the crowds of workers throng-
ing the streets at this time is comparatively slight.
Secondly, the number of older women among these
is very small.

Inquiry at the offices of the two largest interna-
tional unions in these trades confirmed these observations. The proportion of women of all ages to men
in these trades was put at approximately thirty per
cent. They had no figures available giving the number or proportion of older women in this group. But
they were certain that these were relatively small.

The Chief of the Women's Bureau of the New
York State Department of Labor gave it as her opinion that the disinclination of factories to hire middle-
aged women was growing. She considered the higher
group insurance rates for older women the chief reason for this situation. Young workers, too, could usually be obtained for less pay. Employers found them
more agreeable to work with; the older women they
considered set and less amenable to direction.

The head of the Women's Trade Union League

found much the same situation. She summarized the reasons why older women were not much desired in factories as follows: first, because they are slower; secondly, because they are more likely to be ill and thus lose days; thirdly, because they have less muscular control and are therefore more liable to industrial accidents; fourthly, because they are less adaptable; fifthly, because they are more lackadaisical and less careful about their personal appearance; and lastly, because home cares sometimes interfere with the quality and the regularity of their work.

Two of these reasons seem traceable to the nature of the work itself. For instance, the increased tendency to illness and the consequent loss of working days may be due, in the case of older factory workers, to exhaustion resulting from the strain of the work they did at machines in their younger working years. And the lack of care about their personal appearance is quite understandable in view of the fact that it takes at least some leisure to achieve personal neatness. These women, coming home tired out after a hard day only to face household tasks, frequently have no leisure whatever. The last reason stated seems, too, to require some modification. One would expect that younger married women, at any rate, would find home cares very much more of a distraction than older women. It is the younger women who have the helpless small children to guard. Illness among these will frequently cut into the regularity of the young woman's work.

Older women will be employed in factories, then, first, at such work as does not involve any undue strain through speed pressure; secondly, in such plants as are comparatively free from the hazards created by cumbersome machinery rapidly operated; and lastly, in such industries as offer much work that may be done by hand. But in a large proportion of factories, especially in those employing large numbers of workers, the increased group insurance rates for older women previously quoted and the prospect of a too great number of eligibles for pensioning both have considerable weight in determining employment possibilities for them.

V

Older women and work connected with cooking are so closely associated in the average mind that one expects in this field a Mecca of employment for them. And so it may have been in the recent past. But interviews with the employment managers of the three largest chain restaurant systems in New York City show that nowadays there are few places where they can fit in.

Of the three chains chosen, one operates under the name "restaurant company"; one calls its restaurants "tea rooms," although full course dinners are daily served in them; and the third is a cafeteria system.

The employment manager of the restaurant chain

explained that they barred older women only when new waitresses were being considered. The youthful waitresses for whom they advertised were held to be more desirable in that particular work quite as much from the point of view of pleasing the public as from the angle of rendering satisfactory service to the employer. But there were still some middle-aged women to be found as waitresses in their various restaurants —older women who had been with the concern for many years and would be retained as long as they could do the work well. Older women who tried to enter the concern at the present time could be put into the kitchen, to prepare vegetables and to wash dishes.

This chain operates fifty restaurants in Manhattan alone, in each of which there are employed about fifty women. Of these, ten per cent are middle-aged. When any of these older employees becomes eligible for a pension, her case is considered, and disposed of at the option of the company. But the pension problem is not felt to be a very pressing one here, because of the considerable turnover among the employees.

The tea-room chain has a women employment manager. She stated that her concern would not now employ any new women workers above thirty-five or forty years of age for any kind of work whatever. They had in all their branches together about 1,000 women; among those that were middle-aged some had been in their employ for years. These latter worked as supervisors, as waitresses, as matrons, or here and there in the kitchen. Her office tried to find easier work for them when their regular work became too difficult. There was no pension system, but there was a welfare fund in case of illness. Her firm tried to prevent the hiring of women not in good health by giving each new employee a stringent physical test; so that they had comparatively little trouble through illness.

It was pointed out by this manager that because they already had a fair proportion of older women in their employ they had adopted the policy of hiring only young workers for the present. She thought that the older women were less able to stand the strain of restaurant work than younger people, since it required much standing and moving about. She used a sort of preliminary health test of her own on all those who applied to her. She declared that she could tell at a glance the people who suffered from nervous disorders, from poor digestion, or from varicose veins. She had made a study of such things. She could even tell those who had criminal tendencies.

The manager of the cafeteria system explained that although they employed new workers up to forty-five years of age, they would hire none older. They depended on the employees already in their service to fill vacancies that could be covered by older people. He explained that this policy was not actuated by the desire to save insurance rates, because they never had accidents—a fallacious statement, since these rates were paid for protection in case of accident, even though such trouble never occurs. They had in all a force of about 700 women; the number of older women among them he called indefinite. There was no pension system, but there was a welfare fund as in the tea-room chain. The older women they employed peeled potatoes and helped in the kitchen. There were no waitresses, of course; but all those in charge of the passing out of food were young women.

In the restaurants, then, there are not many positions that older women can fill. Serving patrons can usually be done more satisfactorily by young women. Older women who are quick and neat and willing could no doubt do the kitchen work, including the cooking, effectively. But the stream of less efficient older women who probably poured in and out of restaurant kitchens much as they do in and out of the homes have no doubt made it hard for the few who could qualify to get places. Higher group insurance rates and pension fears do not seem to have had much influence in determining policies in these three large chains.

VI

From the employment manager's point of view, then, what qualities possessed by the older woman make her a more desirable employee than the young person? And what qualities make her less desirable?

In all, the opinions of twenty-three employment

managers have here been expressed. They represent many industries; and this variety of interests naturally brings them into contact with many different types of employees, of varying background, training, and capabilities. Yet certain general characteristics seem to have impressed many of them; and these may here be pointed out.

It will have been observed that most of these employment managers, when they considered the desirability of hiring older women, almost automatically divided them into two groups. Of the one they were hardly conscious. These were the workers who in the course of the years had risen out of the ranks to be forewomen, supervisors, heads of departments. Rarely was there any question of their retention, and in most firms they were taken for granted. Where the question of the continuance of an older woman's services came up at all, it was usually in connection with the second group—the routine workers who held the rank-and-file positions. And the matter of filling vacancies related almost exclusively to this latter class.

As to the routine workers, those managers who have mentioned desirable qualities in older women stress their dependability. Older women are steady and faithful on the job; they appear regularly and work earnestly. They are no more troubled by illness as a class than are their younger sisters. There is less turnover among them because, whether from fear or from general inertia, they do not readily give up their positions. They have in most instances acquired a feeling of loyalty to the concern that employs them. They are not apt to ask often for a raise in salary. They are inclined to work resignedly, to put up with conditions, to make the best of things.

Of the undesirable qualities, a tendency to get into a rut and a lack of enthusiasm are often mentioned. But those most frequently and most vehemently objected to are the fact that the older woman is set and not adaptable, and that she is hard to get along with. The older woman will observe that these are largely defects of personality rather than of technical equipment. And she would do well to ponder this fact. For whatever may be the general extent of the employment manager's Biblical knowledge, he appears to be quite familiar with the following:

"It is better to dwell in a desert land,
Than with a contentious and fretful woman."

And he usually shows no hesitancy in demonstrating practically his entire concurrence with the spirit of this quotation.

CHAPTER V

EMPLOYMENT AGENCIES VERSUS THE MIDDLE-AGED WOMEN

I

SOME older women who face the necessity of finding a new position consider registration with employment agencies a more logical means to this end than any other method. Theoretically, they are probably right. The employment agencies have the advantage of knowing both parties to any placement transaction. They are assumed to be expert judges of personnel. One is therefore justified in supposing that here, if anywhere, not only could the older worker find the position best fitted for her, but the business office could find the employee best suited to its needs.

But, in the present imperfect state of general labor adjustments, it rarely happens that the position and the worker who could best fill it are simultaneously available. And, in addition, the situation is often complicated by the putting up of age barriers that must be rigidly adhered to.

Many employers make up their minds not to hire an older woman; to consider only those below twenty-five or thirty for office positions. Yet many women of thirty-five or more, who possess a high degree of intelligence and good taste in dress, present an appearance more fresh and youthful than a girl of twenty who is careless about her dress, her diet, and the hours she keeps. The employer cannot know this fact unless he interviews both applicants. But he himself has blocked his opportunity to obtain the more desirable worker because he has stressed the thing of least importance about any employee—her age. In such instances the placement manager, who may have a well-qualified applicant five or six years older than the limit set, may be powerless to make the adjustment, even though she feels certain that both sides would be satisfied with the result.

The accusation is sometimes made by older women that the employment agencies themselves, rather than the employers, practically close the field of general clerical work to older women. That is doubtful. The agency usually collects as a fee for placing its workers one entire week's salary; and the salaries of older women are often higher than those for younger people in this field. It is hardly likely, therefore, that any agency would deliberately cut into its own financial welfare by any such procedure. It seems safe to assume that, for this one reason alone, placement clerks merely follow orders when they send younger instead of older women to answer calls for office assistants.

There is one type of employment agency that seems to have little difficulty in placing older women. That is the group specializing in the supplying of domestic help. Older women who are neat, agreeable, skilled, and conscientious can readily be placed in homes or in hotels.

This type of work appears to offer a more satisfactory solution of the older woman's employment problem than is possible with similar equipment in any other field. The wages she may earn range from sixty to one hundred dollars a month, including all meals and usually also an attractive room in a much better locality than she can generally choose for herself. The work, requiring as it does a variety of movement, exercises all the muscles during the day, instead of only the set needed in the work at machines or desks. It is therefore much less fatiguing.

Yet, with all these things in their favor, opportunities for obtaining advantageous positions in households often vainly await applicants, while the stream of older women who could fill them turns away toward those agencies that place clerical workers.

Where workers have been engaged in clerical occupations since their early youth, this deflection is comprehensible. They want work in the field that they have made their specialty; that they know they can do well. But many times older women who are just entering industry look for work of this type, in which, even when they do find a position, they can rarely make more than a subsistence wage. Most of these women have had household experience; but, lacking the common sense to use it as a business asset, they gladly accept the most poorly paid routine positions instead.

These women and the older routine clerical workers apply at the agencies for work. A few days of inquiry generally show them two things. First, the offices that place routine workers, and such employers as desire them, usually request young people— that is, workers who are less than twenty-five years old. Secondly, employers whose clerical work is of a type that requires unusual training and initiative prefer, as a rule, women either actually middle-aged or approaching it. Such work is expert bookkeeping; secretarial work requiring educational background; the supervision of a large office; or the exclusive responsibility of a small one.

There are comparatively few such positions; and they are obtained by those older women who have kept pace with the newest developments in their own and its related fields; who have kept track of business trends; who have made themselves masters in some special branch of business practice; who can do a little more just a little better than the average. Such women rarely wait long for a chance to exercise these qualities. For even if no opportunity for them develops from the outside, if no one can find a place for them, they can and do create one for themselves.

But the routine worker who has let the passing years leave her a routine worker still, is indeed at a sorry pass as far as clerical work is concerned. It is very difficult for her to capture such a position in the face of the competition offered her by young women. These are the workers who have had three or four years of clerical experience. They are reinforced by the throngs of young people that pour annually out of the high schools and the privately owned institutions for imparting the technic of routine commercial work. Where routine work is to be done, business offices frankly prefer these young workers. The reasons for this preference are modified by the personality of the prospective employer who desires them; but in general they may be summarized as follows:

1. Younger clerical workers may be obtained at lower salaries than older women—$15 to $18 for beginners as against $20 to $25 for experienced workers.

2. Younger people usually look brighter and fresher in an office, thereby imparting to it an air of briskness not always contributed by older workers.

3. Young employers and office managers do not hesitate to give orders to youthful workers, but dislike to do so in the case of older women.

4. Young people are more adaptable. Older women, especially if they have worked for years with another concern, are apt to have developed one way of doing a thing and adhering fixedly to it in the face of other methods in use in the new office.

5. Younger people are less moody and irritable, and generally easier to get on with.

6. Younger people and older people in the same office, at similar work and at approximately the same salary, do not get on well together. The younger person is likely to feel contempt for the older woman who has not ad-

vanced past her; and the older woman is likely to be envious of a younger person who, in spite of youth, has caught up with her in salary and position.

Not only does the young stenographer or bookkeeper feel superior to the older woman who is only on her level, but the employer, too, is apt to think a little slightingly of her ability. He may consider that, since the technic of such work can be mastered in four or five years, any woman who has not learned more than that must be sadly lacking in initiative. He probably regards her as a woman of little ambition, too easily satisfied, perhaps not too well endowed with ability. He is likely to reason that .did she have any special talents they would long since have rendered her restless and dissatisfied with mere routine work. He may feel that her mental outlook is not likely to broaden with the passing years, while her disposition is likely to sour and her general capacity for work to lessen as time goes by. So, since the market is plentifully supplied with routine workers, he asks for those whose technic he regards as just as well perfected, but who have the added possibilities inherent in youth.

II

What is the service rendered by the employment agency in helping to find positions for the older woman, notably in the field of clerical work? In order

to ascertain approximately the extent of it, the placement managers of twenty-four agencies were interviewed.

In this group are to be found agencies of all types,
from the small one- or two-woman office to the large-
scale organization itself hiring a full staff of employees and engaged in placing thousands of applicants
each week. Most of these supply general clerical
help; four smaller ones have specialized along limited
lines.

Chief among these last, as far as the older woman
is concerned, is one that occupies itself principally
with the supplying of middle-aged clerical help. This
office was opened by a middle-aged woman for this
purpose, after she had vainly tried for some time to
place older women through the regular agencies.
Herself capable and sympathetic, she has been so
successful in her venture that she now has a definite
following of business people who will employ older
women. Most of the workers she places are highly
trained in their various specialties; but she finds employment, too, for older routine workers.

Hers has been a campaign of personal interviews
with employers who at first were desirous of hiring
only young workers, but who finally allowed themselves to be persuaded into trying older women. So
careful was she of the types sent out to fill these positions that in each case the employer was completely won over. Her reputation for the successful handling of this pioneer work is now established with

workers as well as with employers, so that most of the women who come to her for placement are middle-aged.

The second of these agencies specializes in college-trained clerical workers exclusively. In this bureau about one applicant in twelve is an older woman. They are not hard to place if in addition to their academic work they have been well trained along routine commercial lines. There is opportunity for them particularly as social and as executive secretaries.

In the third agency the work is entirely devoted to the placing of part-time clerical and shop assistants. Here about thirty per cent of the applicants are older women. Their chances of obtaining a position through this bureau are fairly good if the applicants have had previous experience and training; otherwise they cannot be placed here.

The last of these specialized agencies is a foreign language bureau; that is, it supplies clerical workers who take dictation in languages other than English, and are also able to carry on business correspondence in these foreign tongues. Sometimes the translation of a commercial work into or out of English is also required. In this bureau only three or four per cent of the applicants are older women; and there are usually good positions waiting for them.

The situation in these bureaus supports the contention already made here and iterated again and again by placement managers in the various agencies —that those women who have made themselves spe-

cialists in a definite field have little difficulty in finding work. Two large-scale offices out of the remaining twenty also support this contention. One of them
is the placement bureau connected with a prominent
institution for training clerical workers in advanced
business practice. As this bureau is situated and well
advertised in the financial district, business concerns
who require expert office assistance have come to
apply to it for workers. The graduates of this institution, many of whom are routine workers desirous
of bettering their position, are then sent out in answer to the calls.

Since many of these positions are of an executive
nature, older women are quite acceptable for filling
them if they are otherwise well qualified. Therefore
the many middle-aged women who apply find no
difficulty in obtaining work if their training has been
of a superior order. Here the placement manager regards the older woman's business chances as entirely
a matter that she has the power to regulate for herself.

The other large-scale office is an ordinary agency
supplying all types of office help. It has, however,
built up contacts especially with publishing houses,
editorial offices of newspapers, educational institutions, and professional people requiring clerical
workers. Since the satisfactory filling of positions
in such organizations frequently requires a mature
person of poise and judgment as well as expert
technical equipment, the older woman who applies

here, if she is of desirable personality and otherwise well trained, is readily placed from this office. About ten per cent of all its registrants are older women; and positions can be found for most of them.

In eleven out of the remaining eighteen, the older applicants also averaged ten per cent of the total workers registering with them; in four, less than nine per cent; and in three the number was indefinite. Fifteen of these agencies declared that they could place no more than one per cent of their middle-aged applicants; one considered the older woman's chances fair; and two said that the number they could place was indefinite.

This group of twenty includes the six leading offices in Manhattan for supplying clerical workers. In one of the largest the arrangements for classifying the workers were unique. The reception office was divided into sections by means of large signs on which appeared the figures: $15, $18, $22, $25. These signs represented the salaries the workers thought they were entitled to earn. The applicants rallied around their respective signposts, where application blanks for registering were then given them. There were usually some older women in each wage group.

At this agency very few positions for older women could be found, although ten per cent of the total registrants were middle-aged. Apparently, then, it is not always because older women must have larger salaries that younger people are sent out instead. Just how well an office can judge the capabilities of its applicants by this method of initial classification is problematical; but since the concern seems to be flourishing, its services in supplying applicants must meet the requirements of many business houses.

Out of these twenty-four offices, then, seven found that they could place their older women registrants advantageously. These applicants amounted to at least ten per cent of all who sought work through them; and nearly all who applied could be placed. The unsuccessful ones failed to find positions not because they were older women, but because they lacked some necessary quality either of personality or of training. But six of these seven offices had made special efforts to serve older women. One ran an agency almost exclusively for them; the others all had special contacts and special work for them to do.

But there were seventeen offices that did not find it easy to place them. This is seventy per cent of the total number investigated. These were the agencies that supply clerical help of a more or less routine character. Fifteen of these could place only about one per cent of the older women who applied to them. These agencies universally disclaimed any responsibility for the situation, saying that they simply did not get calls for older workers. Occasionally they offered to send an older woman; but the firm to whom this offer was made usually did not even grant her an interview.

III

Do older women find it easier to obtain positions through large agencies than through small ones?

Apparently the older women themselves do not think so; for the ten per cent registration ratio for them remains fairly constant for all types of agencies. There are only four outstanding exceptions to this— the foreign language bureau, where the ratio was much smaller; the part-time bureau, the business school placement bureau, and the agency for older women, where the ratio was much larger. Through all of these last, it will be remembered, older women who were well trained found excellent opportunities.

It will be recalled that three out of these four were small agencies who had themselves specialized along definite lines. This would seem to offer an argument in support of the superiority of the small office, were it not for the fact that two of the large agencies who had developed contacts for this purpose also succeeded in placing older women.

Employment agencies, then, serve older women efficiently, not because they are large or small, but when, no matter what the size of the organization, they have made a study of these women's capabilities and have devised ways of marketing them. What has already been done along these lines by a few offices points to infinite further possibilities in those fields.

IV

As has already been pointed out, the fixing of an age barrier at twenty-five or thirty developed first among large-scale organizations that were primarily interested in keeping down all expenses that could possibly reduce dividends. But smaller places, too, have taken up the cry for younger people in offices, probably on the theory that large-scale concerns were experts in business matters, and that therefore whatever they did must have had some excellent basis. The wisdom of drawing these age lines by large corporations, as has already been indicated, is seriously open to question from the point of view of lowering their expenses, because the loss from the large turnover among young workers—averaging sixty per cent and costing approximately $29 for each separation*—is likely to overbalance any saving. But even assuming that their practice in this matter is sound, what is good policy for an organization of this type may be quite the wrong one for a concern employing only three or four clerical workers. Yet even the office requiring only one stenographer echoes, according to the employment agencies, this cry for young clerical workers.

The following letter is reprinted from the New York *Sun* of January 7th, 1928. It is one of many that have appeared intermittently in the daily press

---

* "Suggestions for Selling Group Insurance." Equitable Life Assurance Society, pp. 12–14.

during the past two years, all of them illustrations
of the situation we have been discussing.

TOO OLD AT 35?

ONE WOMAN HAS HAD TROUBLE IN FINDING WORK.

To the What Do You Think Editor—

Sir: I would like to submit the following question:

What is a woman 35 years of age to do? I am a capable
stenographer, well dressed (but not flashily), look thirty,
but have been turned down time and again because employers have drawn the dead line at twenty-five. Banks,
particularly, which set no age limit in accepting deposits,
will not employ a girl over twenty-five. Agencies have
told me "we do not register any one thirty or over."

Is a woman of my age to take chloroform, as our friend
Osler suggested?   THIRTY-FIVE.

This stenographer appears to have been particularly unfortunate in her choice of agencies at which
to apply; for none of the twenty-four here considered refused to register older women, even if fifteen
of them could hope to place only about one per cent
of those they entered. The situation indicated in her
letter is serious enough for her. But one is led to wonder whether banks that pursue the policy of hiring
only young workers do not also suffer somewhat by
so doing. Will they not find it something of a boome-
rang? The chief asset of a bank is public confidence.
It is doubtful whether the effect on the public of
these immature, youthful clerks and stenographers

is one of dependability and stability. Its customers may come to feel that, in intrusting its work to these lower priced and less experienced employees, these banks are not taking the financial affairs of its patrons seriously enough.

V

As far as the older woman is concerned, then, there is much that the privately run agency can do to place her that has not, thus far, been very extensively attempted. Because these agencies are not fully able to meet the situation, bureaus run by the State or by the municipality are often suggested to supplement them. Would such offices be of any greater service to her?

New York State conducts a public employment bureau, with a special department for women. Here about one hundred women, many of whom are middle-aged, call daily in an attempt to find work. Where they can do chamberwork or are efficient at any other type of domestic service they can be placed through this office in institutions, hotels, or restaurants. They are also frequently desired for part-time household positions, and for night office cleaning. But there are practically no calls for them from either factories or business offices. The clerical worker and the factory worker are as much at a disadvantage in applying here as they are in the privately run agencies.

How far does the bureau now run by the State approximate the usefulness it might attain? Whatever may be the degree of its service in other fields, as an aid to older women looking for clerical or factory work it leaves much to be desired. Here is a problem concerning the employment of women in these occupations—fields extending into many industries and therefore requiring hundreds of thousands of workers. Women over thirty-five, sometimes even younger, find great difficulty in entering them, not because of the type of serious industrial dislocation that often causes widespread worklessness, but because of something far less tangible and therefore harder to combat. She is denied work because of an idea—a theory that age must be the measure of a woman's industrial value.

Does the bureau study the problem with a view to ameliorating this situation? Just what does it do to help dissipate the cloud that hangs so threateningly over women who, by all the standards set by physicians and psychologists, still have their most productive years ahead of them? Most private agencies fail to place older women in these fields to any appreciable extent. The public agency fails even worse. Where, on the basis of this showing, would an argument for more public agencies find support?

The public agency does not meet the situation at present because it is run largely as a routine bureau. It does not operate on the theory that it is an economic factor making employment adjustments for its own citizens better than any private agency could hope to do it. Until it does, it can make only the surface adjustments that the private agencies usually make. The fact that it does not charge a fee is the only point of difference—one hardly great enough to be a real public service.

That it does not function better is not because the people operating it are wilfully unsympathetic. Quite the contrary. As far as they go, they try to find work for as many people who apply as possible. The head of the woman's division, in attempting to assign causes for the older woman's plight, will tell you, as so many employment managers have already done, that older women have somehow acquired a reputation for not being pliable. Then, too, there are many young people in places of authority, and they do not like to ask older women to do things for them. Moreover the older women, especially if inexperienced, are inclined to be particular about the jobs they will take. She is very sorry for the situation. Probably there is not very much that she herself can do. The trouble comes in accepting as inevitable a condition that tends to work injury to older women, instead of devising means to combat it. As the matter now stands, when a public bureau cannot place clerical workers and factory workers who come to it, because they are older women, does it not to just that extent fail to function in its field of articulating workers and suitable positions? And should not effort be bent toward the evolving of methods that will overcome this missing effectiveness?

A State employment system has some of the same angles of importance for the general public as those presented by a public-school system. The essence of the success of both lies in their ability to serve groups by serving individually each person in them. It is only when a State agency begins to approach its serious task with a full realization of its importance and its possibilities that we can hope for better services in the employment field not only from the State agency itself but from the privately run agencies as well. At present the older woman derives very limited assistance from the State agency—far less, in fact, than from the small agencies that have specialized in her needs, and have learned to market her resources successfully.

VI

A consideration of the agency problem demonstrates that, contrary to the belief held by some older women, the employment bureaus do not deliberately hold back the middle-aged registrants who come to them for clerical positions. They keep a shop for services; and certain of these services are demanded by their customers—the business offices—just as certain goods are preferred in any other shop. Like all other firms they try to supply the type of service requested. At present the demand, especially for clerical workers, is sharply in favor of young people.

The older woman has never been a favorite in business offices. In the days of her commercial beginnings most of the women who became clerical workers did so as a temporary expedient until marriage delivered them from it. Those women who did not marry were for the most part regarded askance, partly because they did not choose or find a husband, and partly because they were still content to serve as routine workers. In those days, when the young office worker married, there was rarely any doubt in her mind that such a step involved the resignation of her position in the office; and so the labor turnover was then even greater, comparatively speaking, than it is now. Then business men illogically scolded in one breath the young women for being only temporary factors in industry, and the older women because they seemed to be permanent.

Some of the ancient prejudice against the older woman in business offices may have carried over into the present. But to it have been added certain economic factors, such as higher salaries, higher group insurance rates, and the fact that many offices require only an elementary type of routine work that can be done fairly well by young workers.

A brief conversation may be reported in illustration of the general attitude in this field toward older women. A young woman under thirty, whose business requires the services of several stenographers, was asked if she would not hire women over thirty-five for such work.

"No," she replied, "they'd probably be too high-priced. I've just put in a girl of twenty who's quite expert enough for my purposes. And she gets a beginner's salary."

"Suppose an older woman were willing to accept that. Would you take her?"

"Well, no. She might get on my nerves."

The questioner mentioned several girls in the young woman's employ that occasionally possessed that capacity.

"Yes, that's true," was the reply. "It depends on personality."

Exactly. It depends on personality, which at any age may be desirable or the reverse.

This attitude of mind is only too common among employers. The net result is that business offices demand young workers, and that the agencies as a rule, without attempting to question its wisdom or fairness, meet this demand.

Agencies, in order to serve the public effectively, need urgently to advance from the mere routine offices many of them now are to intelligently run markets for labor exchange. But if the older woman on her part is to derive full benefit from such improved employment aids, she must develop into as expert a worker as possible. She is lost among the mass of routine workers if she has advanced no further herself. But, if better trained than they, she would shoulder above them. If she does nothing to develop her capabilities to the fullest extent she must not complain if, permitting herself to be undistinguished, she is suffered by industry to remain so.

Even more important for the older woman than a fully trained technic is a desirable personality. There is no reason why an employer need tolerate a person who is rude, cross, generally unpleasant, and careless about her personal appearance—whatever her age. But he is considerably more apt to resent these things in an older than in a younger woman, and to show it in no uncertain way.

The employer often hampers the work of the agency by making his first requirement, particularly in clerical work, the youth of the applicant. A woman of twenty-six-or-seven has not suddenly lost since her twenty-fifth birthday all the charm, the energy, the capability, that distinguished her a year or so earlier. As a matter of fact, she probably not only retains them, but has intensified them even at ten or fifteen years older, provided she is a normal human being able to profit by life's experiences.

The employer often stands in his own light as well by erecting these age barriers. It is extremely difficult to judge a woman's age by her appearance, especially in this day of bobbed hair and youthful styles in dress. The woman who comes to him acknowledging that she has lived twenty-three-or-four years may easily have forgotten an extra ten or fifteen years as far as he is able to judge. He may, therefore, be hiring a middle-aged woman in spite of all his precautions; but one who is not above deceiving him. Would it not be better, since he cannot in any event be sure of the age of his applicants, if he were to throw age barriers entirely aside, and let the agencies send him workers of desirable personality and training, regardless of every other consideration?

Were the employer to withdraw age lines, the public, including older women, would be in a much better position to judge the attitude of the agencies with regard to age limits. As the matter now stands, it appears to resolve itself into the following conclusions:

1. Agencies that have the services of well qualified older women to offer, and who have made the proper contacts, have little difficulty in finding work for them.

2. Agencies that have a more or less indifferent attitude toward older women, that have neglected to make contacts of a helpful nature in placing them, and that have accepted the qualifications made by employers without question, cannot place them successfully.

Insofar as the latter agencies do not completely realize their possibilities they are to blame for the older woman's predicament. Some of her plight is due to the attitude of employers. Some of it is unquestionably the fault of the older woman herself. In this industrial triangle, there is much to be said on all sides. But let us assume for a moment that the various factors in it were to be judged by an impartial committee on which were no representatives of agencies, no employers of clerical workers, no older women looking for work. After the arguments on all sides were duly weighed, which would be chosen as the side having the most logic and justice to support it?

PART II
THE PROBLEM ANALYZED

CHAPTER I

THE MIDDLE–AGED WOMAN'S PART IN IT

I

We have watched in the preceding chapters the functioning of the various media through which the older woman must pass in looking for employment. Newspaper advertisements help her but little. Employment agencies do not welcome her or, as a rule, care to help her. Personnel offices protect their inmost sanctums in many cases through clerks who turn faces of adamant in the direction of older women looking for work.

In this drama of the older woman in industry one would expect her to have a leading rôle. But those other characters have stronger parts. They are in a much better position to affect her than she is to influence them. Each of them plays the part of a road that she must traverse. But, as all roads used to lead to Rome, so now do all these lead most older women seeking work to the stone wall of age barriers.

Sometimes she protests against the minor part assigned to her. But such outbreaks are generally ineffective because they dwindle down to a few loose-end meetings or sporadic epistolary outbreaks in the newspapers. Neither of these things will much impress the director. She must make him see the nature of the cruelty that lies in condemning to commercial impotency women in the first years of their maturity. She must make him understand the seriousness of what he is doing in placing in her path a wall that must forever block her work unless he himself tear it down. She must convince him that, by leaving it there, he is not only dealing her a mortal blow, but hurting himself financially as well, and, through these two injuries, the whole of society.

The forces pitted against the older woman threaten to overpower her and to make her attainment of a stellar rôle most doubtful for the present. Yet she is numerically great enough to be given a place of industrial importance. Middle-aged workers form a considerable segment of the gainfully employed women of the city. The Fourteenth Federal Census gives figures on the basis of which the number in only five occupations* for Greater New York alone was computed at 196,538, or 32 per cent of the working women of the city. For Manhattan Borough alone the number, computed on a similar basis, is 111,448, or 37 per cent of the total of working women in it.

Figure IX shows graphically the number of women workers twenty-five years of age and older in the four important industries we have been considering, in comparison with the number of women of all ages engaged in them.

In the manufacturing industries, which includes

* Saleswomen, clerks and packers counted as one.

all types of factory work, 23,084 women, or 11.3 per cent of all those engaged in them in New York City, are forty-five years of age or older. If we accept the

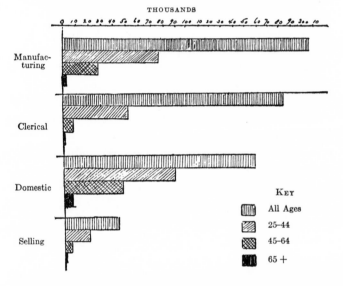

FIGURE IX

NUMBER AND AGE OF WOMEN IN FOUR GREAT INDUSTRIES, GREATER NEW YORK

Data from Fourteenth Federal Census, Vol. 9, Occupations

strictures of some concerns and make the age of twenty-five the limit of employability, the addition of the whole twenty-five to forty-four group, or 37 per cent of all factory workers, brings the number of women in manufacturing in Greater New York who are considered older women from the employers' standpoint, to 48.3 per cent. If, however, the age of thirty-five be considered the starting-point of middle age, one-half the twenty-five to forty-four group brings the total percentage of older women in manufacturing to only 29.8 per cent.

In similar fashion we find that in the selling field* 3,339 women, or 8.4 per cent of all the women engaged in this work in the city, are forty-five years old or more. The addition of the whole twenty-five to forty-four year group, 16,026 more, brings the percentage of women in this work to 49 per cent. Of these approximately 28.7 per cent are thirty-five years old or older.

Clerical work shows the smallest number of older women as workers. Only 5,203 women, or 2.8 per cent of all the vast army of 184,598 clerical workers in Greater New York, are forty-five years old or more. The addition of the 51,535 women in the twenty-five to forty-four year group brings this percentage to 30.7. Of these approximately 16.7 per cent are thirty-five years old or more.

It is in the field of domestic work that the older woman is most frequently to be found. 46,945 women, or 29.9 per cent of all the workers in this field, are at least forty-five years old. With the addition of the twenty-five to forty-four year group this percentage rises to 84.1 per cent. If we consider only those over thirty-five years of age, it still remains quite high—57 per cent.

Figure X shows similar conditions for Manhattan

* Including clerks.

Borough alone. Here, again, it is domestic work that leads in the percentage of older women employed.

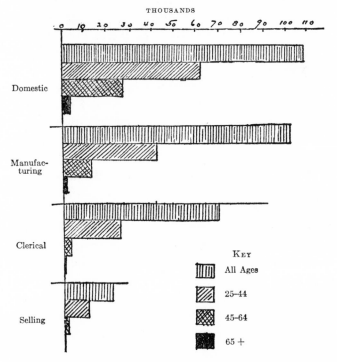

FIGURE X

NUMBER AND AGE OF WOMEN IN FOUR GREAT INDUSTRIES, MANHATTAN BOROUGH

Data from Fourteenth Federal Census, Vol. 9, Occupations

THOUSANDS

KEY

All Ages	
25–44	
45–64	
65 +	

The number who are at least forty-five years old is here 29,449, or 27.6 per cent of all the women domestic workers. These, together with the 60,463 women in the twenty-five to forty-four year group make 84.5 per cent over twenty-five years old. The percentage of women thirty-five years old or older approximates 56.1 per cent.

Manufacturing engages the time of 11,963 women of forty-five or over, or 11.9 per cent of all the women factory workers in the borough. The addition of the twenty-five to forty-four year group makes the percentage of women twenty-five years old or older 51.6 per cent, and those of thirty-five or older approximately 31.8 per cent.

In salesmanship, for the 1,543 women at least forty-five years old the percentage is 8.5. Adding 7,935 workers—the group between twenty-five and forty-four years old—we obtain 52.2 per cent for all saleswomen at least twenty-five years old, and approximately 30.3 per cent for those at least thirty-five years of age.

Clerical work once again makes the poorest showing as far as the older woman is concerned. Only 2,443 out of 66,254 women, or 3.6 per cent, are forty-five years or older. The number in the twenty-five to forty-four year group is 20,971, which brings the percentage of clerical workers twenty-five years old or more to 35.3. The percentage for those thirty-five years old or more is approximately 19.5 per cent.

In considering the figures from the Fourteenth Federal Census on which these graphs and percentages are based, it must be borne in mind that the situation regarding middle-aged women has changed somewhat since the census figures were compiled.

The openly expressed preference for young workers manifested by some large-scale concerns is a comparatively new development. The results to the older woman that it has brought about will be reflected accurately only after the census to be taken in 1930 has been completed. Yet the 1920 figures pointed out some trends that, had the older woman but recognized them in time, might have made her employment problems easier to solve.

The percentages in Figure XI for clerical workers, for instance, clearly reflect the fact that in this field the woman in her forties is not much in evidence. It would be most interesting were it possible to discover why the 68.3 per cent of clerical workers that represents the number of all women younger than twenty-five years of age in this work in Manhattan dwindled to only 31.7 per cent for the women in the twenty-five to forty-four year group, and became a bare 3.6 per cent after the age of forty-five. Do these workers change much to other fields? Do they drop out after twenty-five because they marry and keep house? Do many of them advance to executive positions? Are they discharged as they grow nearer the twenty-five year mark, and are they thus compelled to readjust themselves to other occupations because no one will hire them in their own work? It is difficult to decide which of these questions covers the largest number of cases. But the very fact that so small a percentage is to be found in the field after forty-five years of age, should give the clerical worker

FIGURE XI

PERCENTAGE OF WOMEN 25 YEARS OLD AND
OVER IN FOUR GREAT INDUSTRIES

Based on Data from Fourteenth Federal Census, Vol. 9, Occupations

MANHATTAN BOROUGH

Occupations	Total No., All Ages	25–44	45+	Total, 25 or Over	Total, 35 or Over
Domestic........	106,330	56.9	27.6	84.5	56.1
Manufacturing..	99,722	39.6	11.9	51.6	31.8
Selling.........	18,147	43.7	8.5	52.2	30.3
Clerical........	66,254	31.7	3.6	35.3	19.5

ALL NEW YORK CITY

Occupations	Total No., All Ages	25–44	45+	Total, 25 or Over	Total, 35 or Over
Domestic........	156,667	54.2	29.9	84.1	57.0
Manufacturing..	204,129	37.0	11.3	48.3	29.8
Selling.........	39,469	40.6	8.4	49.0	28.7
Clerical........	184,598	27.9	2.8	30.7	16.7

In the above, the totals for ages 35 and over were found by taking one-half of the 25–44 year group and adding to those 45 and over.

pause. Apparently it is not a field in which the older woman has so far found many opportunities. The observations made in other parts of this study confirm this finding.

On the other hand, the percentage of domestic workers who are at least forty-five years of age is 27.6. In this type of work a total of only 15.5 per cent of all the women engaged are younger than twenty-five years old. Since, as has already been pointed out, the work is well paid and has many other advantages, it would appear to be a sensible course for older women who like housework to prepare themselves for expert service in it. If the women who hire domestic workers could be trained to regard the engagement of such help as a business matter, governed by the same principles, including the question of hours, that prevail in other fields, it is quite likely that many a woman would turn to this work rather than to the factory or to the office. As matters stand at present two large groups—those who engage domestic workers and those older women whose services they might otherwise obtain—both suffer because housewives as well as possible domestic workers do not realize all the possibilities inherent in co-operating with each other.

In the selling field 52.2 per cent, or more than half the women engaged in it, are over twenty-five years old. Here the personality of the employee is so important an element both in her success and in that of her employer that it is doubtful if even those shops who are at present beginning the system of installing only young workers will long continue to do so. In factory work also the percentage of women over twenty-five years old is slightly more than half, or 51.6 per cent of all the women engaged in it. In both groups, however, the bulk of the women older than twenty-five are in the group between that age and forty-four years. Only comparatively small percentages are found above the latter age. The percentages for New York City as a whole follow generally the tendencies pointed out in connection with the situation for Manhattan Borough only.

For all four occupations considered in Figure XI the percentage of women over thirty-five is 34.4 for Manhattan and 33 for all Greater New York. These figures correspond quite closely with the 37 per cent for Manhattan and the 32 per cent for all New York City found in Figures VII and VIII, when the numbers for the transportation industry and packing were included.

Yet, in spite of these large numbers and percentages, the middle-aged woman is just now practically a passive agent as far as determining the conditions of her employment is concerned. She will probably remain so until the forces that now oppose her, better realizing the effects of their strictures not only on her but on themselves, withdraw some of the handicaps that hamper her opportunities.

II

The fact that the middle-aged woman's personality is sometimes cited as the chief ground for the failure of some firms to give her employment has before been mentioned. What is her personal contribution to the complications of her employment problem? How do her personality and her home surroundings affect her chances of finding work? It will be easier to arrive at some conclusions regarding these questions, if we again reclassify older women, this time along three lines—background, temperament, and family obligations.

Fortunate indeed is that older woman whose home environment in her formative years was kindly, sympathetic, intelligent, and wisely thoughtful. To-day she reaps the benefit of the careful training she enjoyed in her youth; for she faces the business world unafraid, trained along the lines best suited to her capabilities. She is pleasant and gracious of manner because her nerves were not continually jangled by an atmosphere of bickering and faultfinding. She is alert mentally because she has constantly heard the questions of the day discussed at home—and that without rancor. She is careful of her personal appearance as a matter of course.

But many other women have been less fortunate. If the homes of their youth were lacking in graciousness, in a desire for mental development, in the niceties that are the standards of the mores of to-day, their bearing reflects this lack. Commercial handicaps often ensue.

It is not impossible to overcome defects of early training and environment if the will to do so be sincere. Many women do it successfully. But others go on, blindly wondering why place after place refuses them employment, when the difficulty may be caused by awkward details of dress or of manner that could easily be righted were these women but conscious of them.

The cruel element in the situation is that very frequently they are not. Robert Burns's wish uttered so long ago—

> "Oh wad some Power the giftie gie us
> To see ourself as ithers see us!
> It wad frae mony a blunder free us,
> And foolish notion."

still often goes unfulfilled.

While careful home training is certainly an aid to her success throughout the older woman's business career, it has here been mentioned chiefly because of the favorable first impression it makes on prospective employers. A position once secured, another factor steps in to modify the situation—to wit, the matter of temperament.

Cheerfulness as a business asset has so often been emphasized that, in the desire to achieve it, irritating exaggerations, such as Pollyannism, slap-on-the-back hail-fellow-well-metism, and stereotyped smiles have sometimes resulted. While such insincerities are obviously undesirable, the older woman whose cheerfulness arises out of natural optimism and gaiety of spirit is indeed fortunate. If added to a sunny temperament she has warm, quick sympathies and the ready smile that expresses these, she may grow older to her heart's content. But sometimes older women are depressed, moody, and irritable. They are quick to take offense, and apt to hold grudges. They make no attempt to be pleasant to their associates. They are victims of an unfortu nate temperament, and to that extent they deserve sympathy. But do they deserve employment?

The woman who is hindered commercially neither by her manner nor by her temperament may have family obligations that retard her progress. Where these home worries continue for any length of time, they may eventually prove a real detriment to her career.

The older woman, then, contributes liberally to her own lack of success if she fails to realize her shortcomings, or, knowing them, lacks the determination to overcome them. She carries her own commercial indictment with her if she makes no attempt to counteract any tendency she may have to be sour and gloomy of disposition. She closes the door to her own commercial advancement if she fails to keep growing mentally. She places stumbling-blocks in her own path if she neglects her health and her personal appearance.

But she is the victim of circumstances when home cares that she is too conscientious to deny call on her physical reserves to such an extent that for the time being she is not as efficient commercially as she might be. Nor can she be blamed if she fails to obtain a position because, when she applies for it, she finds erected against her a blind wall of prejudice that sternly bars out all older women.

III

Two recently published newspaper articles reflect so well the current commercial opinion regarding older women in industry that they may here be cited. One appeared in the New York *Sunday Times* of September 27, 1927. It was headed:

YEARS PROVE HANDICAP TO WOMEN IN BUSINESS

Especially in Secretarial Work the Young Are in Demand, Employment Agencies Find—But Personality and Ability Count Heavily.

This article gives interveiws with two employment agency directors, one of whom heads the employment work of the well-known philanthropic organization earlier mentioned in connection with the Brooklyn protest meeting of older workers. Since neither agency was among those visited for this study, a few of their views are here outlined:

1. Both the women interviewed concur in the opinion that youth and personal appearance score heavily in favor of applicants for clerical work.

2. Both feel that older women in clerical work who have been "unsuccessful" have only themselves to blame. They did not look ahead.

One thinks that secretarial posts can be "perfectly well" filled by young workers.

The director of the welfare employment office finds that lack of youth is not an "insuperable barrier" to obtaining a position if the applicant has other "personal qualifications." What these are she does not state. But both directors—and this is important— feel that, while there may be exceptions here and there, the woman in her thirties who is still looking for a clerical position is a failure.

Nothing could be more unjust. The mere fact that an older woman is trying to find a new post is very poor evidence indeed on which to condemn her as "unsuccessful." If success is to be measured by one's ability to stay put, then the barnacle would be a shining example of success. The older woman in quest of work may be looking for a new secretarial place for the very reason that her old one offered her nothing better than to remain *in statu quo*. The very thing that these directors stigmatize as "unsuccessful" may be ambition. Moreover, conditions in offices are not always ideal. There may have been irritating influences at work in the one where she was employed that made it quite impossible for her to continue and still preserve her self-respect. Then, too, reorganization of her firm may have released an excellent secretary for new work. Ill health or home duties or sudden grief may have forced her to resign for a time and then to go back into industry to begin anew. These are only a few of the reasons which may have been the cause of the older woman going the rounds of the agencies looking for "secretarial jobs." To say, as one of these directors does, that for the most part she is not "qualified for anything better" is to stigmatize at the same time the work and the worker.

There is reflected in this attitude the unfortunate idea too often current especially among us as a nation, that success is measured by the amount of power and money one can accumulate. A belief in that notion ought to make of us a melancholy and discouraged people; for only comparatively few can rise to places of eminence in those fields. Does that necessarily mean that those who do well the work they have chosen and for which they are fitted are "unsuccessful" because that work yields them neither much money nor any power? Is a woman who has perfected herself as a secretary and who likes the work and wishes to remain in this field "unsuccessful" because she is content thus to continue? She may realize that the achievement of expertness in secretarial work measures the extent of her commercial ability; and, since that is so, that she is wiser to be a good secretary than to reach out for a position that she can fill but indifferently. This may not be a very ambitious point of view. But the very fact that she is thus capable of self-analysis is a strong argument in favor of her value to any concern that hires her; for it indicates both a desire to do her utmost and a shrewd estimate of the limitations of her ability.

Considering her a failure may in some cases operate as a decided factor in making her one. It is only the rare older woman who can preserve faith in herself against constantly recurring employment rejections because of her age. Only a strong character can survive repeated statements that she is unsuccessful and still make good. When the effects of such statements strike at the very roots of an older woman's chance for self-support, whence is to come her self-possession on entering an office for an interview? How can her manner reflect a hope that she may prove desirable when that hope is non-existent because it has been killed by repeated batterings against the stone barriers of age limits?

It is equally erroneous to say that secretarial work can be done "perfectly well" by a young applicant. That may be so in some cases. But the reason for it would be neither the youth of the applicant nor the rudimentary character of the work. It would only be because she possesses unusual ability. The average young worker, as has before been stated, lacks the experience necessary to perfect the mechanism of her work. She has not yet had time to acquire mature judgment. She may have instinctive tact; but tact takes years of experience to function at its best. It would be far more accurate to say that the average young worker is able to fill "well enough" the duties of secretary in an office where perfection is not considered essential, where the work is routine in character, and where most of her thinking is done for her. Even in such places the older woman's stability would be more valuable in the long run. She is usually not of a smaller caliber personally than the average young worker. To be sure, she is not, as a rule, as decorative; and in offices where decoration rather than efficient service is the prime consideration she is therefore distinctly at a disadvantage.

This article from *The Times* has here been considered at some length, not because it is in itself particularly valuable, but because it is a good example of the unfair thinking and the loose estimates that are working against middle-aged women to-day in their effort to gain a foothold in industry. On the surface, the statements made in it are plausible enough; and the average employer, reading them cursorily, is not likely to delve below them. Unconsciously, though, such statements influence adversely his point of view regarding older women. That is why they work so much harm. The middle-aged woman must bear the brunt of this silently forming erroneous opinion.

In contrast to the article just reviewed let us consider the second, which appeared in the New York *Sunday World* for September 18, 1927. Here the employment manager of a large department store expresses his views on the hiring of older women. He was not included in the list of those interviewed for this study because his opinions had already been so plainly set forth in this article. It is headed:

Women in the Thirties Are Best Business Bets; When Younger They Wed; When Older They Grieve.

In the course of the interview this manager outlines with keen insight the various advantages and disadvantages to a shop in hiring workers of various ages. He finds that the great difficulty with women under thirty who have business ability is the fact that they are apt to give up their positions for marriage just when their experience has reached the point where the store can reap the benefit of having trained them. The women just entering middle age, on the other hand, are apt to take their business careers seriously and, even though they marry, to remain with the firm. He feels that married women can successfully carry both home and shop work because modern improvements in the home give them much leisure time, and because store hours are so arranged that the two can be dovetailed very easily.

As to the woman over forty, he does not bar her. He even points out the fact that some women who started after that age without previous business experience rose to the top of their fields. But he feels that as a rule those women over forty who are still in routine positions are apt to lose hope; and that the quality of their work is apt to reflect their discouragement.

This is a debatable point, though it is undoubtedly true in some instances. But the many older women that do their work cheerfully and enthusiastically even after they have had to celebrate their fortieth birthday, discount it as a blanket statement. Still, it cannot be denied that some women who hold routine positions after middle age do sink to the feeling that they may now settle back securely for the rest of their lives. Sometimes they cease to put forth further effort, and regard each day's work as a stint that is to be accomplished with as little expenditure of energy as possible. Such tendencies are indeed danger signals; and the older woman who fails to heed them in time is headed for the disaster of unemployment; for she can no more remain static than can any other living organism. If she does not struggle to keep at least on the level she has already reached, she must inevitably slip back. The curbing of such tendencies and the avoidance of the consequences of allowing them to develop, lie in her own hands.

The store employment manager ends his article with this statement regarding age preferences:

"But such preconceived opinions can always be overcome by ability and industry of the woman who is determined to succeed."

If all employment managers were equally fair, many of the older woman's problems would be solved. It will be observed that, since he neither raises age barriers himself nor advocates their erection, the able older woman without business experience—or with it, for that matter—has the opportunity to contribute her powers to industry and at the same time to realize her own possibilities.

The two points of view represented in these articles form an interesting contrast. Unfortunately for the older woman, the first is by far the more prevalent.

IV

The opinion is sometimes held by the older woman that, because so many young workers retain their positions after marriage, her own employment chances are lowered. Is this true?

The director of the Women's Bureau of the United States Department of Labor, in her report for 1926, says concerning married women in industry:

"Census figures show that over three quarters of the married women were in manufacturing and mechanical industries, domestic and personal service, and agriculture —types of work in which women have almost no opportunity for a career. It would appear, therefore, that economic necessity and not the desire to earn 'pin money' or to escape household drudgery is responsible for their gainful employment."

That leaves one-quarter of the number of married working women for the selling, clerical, and similar occupations. Although there is more chance of a career here than in the other fields mentioned, it is hardly great enough to account for all the salespeople and clerical workers who retain their positions after marriage. The comparative ease with which modern housekeeping can be carried on has several times been mentioned; and this unquestionably accounts for part of the situation. Love of luxury and the desire to buy material comforts not possible on the husband's salary no doubt contribute some portion. Economic necessity probably accounts for most of the remainder.

If, then, some of these women find it necessary to support themselves either wholly or in part, or if their earnings are needed in the support of members of their family, the fact that they are married can hardly be made a bar to their employment. They are forced to enter the economic struggle just as are the older women who are dependent on their own efforts for sustenance. They do swell the total number of available workers in each age group and in each industry; and to that extent competition increases for any positions open. But in some industries employers prefer not to hire married women at any age for fear that their home duties may hinder their economic efficiency. In others, especially in those where young workers are preferred, it is youth and not the marital status of the worker that turns the decision against the older woman. It must be admitted that, were all married women to withdraw from industry, the resulting shortage of labor would undoubtedly give unmarried older women more employment opportunities. But it would at the same time close the doors of employment to older women who happen to be married. These may conceivably have an invalid husband to support, or near relatives to help. Therefore the result would be a shifting of evils rather than their eradication.

It is quite as unfair for older women to expect that young married workers be excluded from industrial competition with them as it is for any one else to erect any other artificial barriers to the free operation of the labor market. Positions should be given to those best qualified personally and technically to fill them, irrespective of age, marital status, or religion. That seems to be the basis upon which the greatest industrial return for all the elements concerned in production can best be secured.

V

Why did so many of the present-day older routine workers come into industry so little equipped to advance? In order better to understand that phase of our problem we must go back to the schools as they existed in New York City twenty-five or thirty years ago.

The high schools of that day were neither as diversified nor as numerous as they are at present. Where now girls may choose to attend a commercial high school, a school for the study of textile design and manufacture, a manual training high school, or an academic high school, according to their several needs and desires, their elders were expected to attend secondary schools only if they were going on from them either to a normal school or to college.

For those who were expected to enter commercial life, the ordinary grammer school education, which then consisted of eight years of general elementary training, was considered ample preparation. Indeed, many of the girls of a generation ago who started their careers in the shops as cash girls did not attend beyond the first five or six years of this course.

Those who remained until they received diplomas at the end of the eight years' course were the brighter students. Of these, some who were not considered clever enough by their parents to become teachers were, however, sent on to a "business school" to learn rudimentary bookkeeping, typewriting and stenography. A course of this kind usually took six months to complete, after which the girl, at perhaps fourteen or fifteen years old, was considered well enough equipped to adorn any business office.

But many times parents did not regard even that meagre amount of preparation to be necessary before their children entered commercial life. Frequently these young people, immediately following their elementary schooling, were sent out into some firm to "make themselves generally useful," or perhaps to become "bright beginners, paid while learning," with some milliner or dressmaker. The old grammar school course took no cognizance of the needs of business as such, but devoted itself to the imparting of a knowledge of reading, writing, arithmetic, formal grammar; history in the shape of the chief battles of our various wars, the date of their happening, and the generals and the number killed and wounded on each side; geography that considered chiefly the capitals of the States, with the rivers on which they were situated; and literature that included the parroting of "memory gems" and "quotations." As it was felt in those days that a book must have the sanction of posterity before it could be considered as food for young minds, the works of the day were severely neglected. Newspaper reading was not encouraged in the schools; a little sheet briefly outlining the important happenings of the day was felt to be exciting enough for children to read.

Most of the middle-aged routine workers of to-day are the products of such schools. But so, also, are many of the executives who hire and fire them. Why do some "fish," as a famous professor at Columbia University remarked long ago, while these routine workers merely "cut bait"? Differences in native ability and in home environment account for some of it. Differences in the extent of their will to succeed and in their ability to measure and to keep pace with improvements in their work, account for more of it.

The old schools may not always have been stimulating to the intelligence, but their product—these older women who are the routine workers of to-day —did learn to calculate accurately, to read fluently, to spell correctly. They were, too, fortunate enough to grow up in a generation when the worst features of modern journalism were yet undreamed of. And they had the further advantage of passing their industrial novitiate at the time when "big business" was just beginning to develop along its present lines, and when the personnel of such concerns was recognized to be a vital element in aiding in their growth. Employees were encouraged to remain long with a firm. Firms, in their turn, prided themselves on being able to inspire loyal service on the part of their workers.

The middle-aged women who have back of them this industrial experience have inevitably acquired some valuable characteristics. They have learned thoroughly the limited things the schools taught them; and, going from these into industry, they have acquired respect for loyal service and the value of it to their firms. Some of them, even though they did not take advantage of the courses in advanced work in the evening high schools that were just beginning to be introduced a generation or so ago, still made themselves so mechanically perfect through their long experience that they are to-day like highly tempered machines in their field.

The limited scope of elementary schooling, the fact that the high schools were then in their infancy, and the added point that industry itself used to be considered the best place in which to begin business training, account for the comparatively poor educational background possessed by some older routine workers.

Let us see how the young workers of to-day compare with them in these points.

In the first place, the modern girl who chooses to

enter industry comes to it from all types of homes. Industry is to-day recognized as offering opportunities for careers to an extent undreamed of a quarter of a century ago. Furthermore, the "home girl" is now practically extinct; girls as well as boys usually plan nowadays to undertake some definite career.

Industry, too, is to-day much more complex than it was a generation ago; no girl who expects to succeed now can hope to enter a firm at fourteen or fifteen to be "generally useful." She realizes that she cannot hope to progress in industry unless she comes to it with something definite to offer. And even if she were to try, here in New York State the new education law* would step in her path. For according to its terms girls as well as boys must attend school for at least part of the day until they are seventeen. If they have completed a minimum course they need attend continuation school but four hours a week. Even that meagre amount is bound to result in some mental stimulation. But, better than that, the law usually operates to give a considerable number of young people a portion at least of the city high school course. Many of them complete the entire course of four years before they enter industry.

Have these superior educational facilities eliminated the routine worker or insured commercial success for all our young people? It would indeed be hopeful were this so. But one strong reason operates against it—namely, the fact that superior ability is

*Passed in 1920.

a rare thing, and that no amount of schooling can create it where it does not already exist. It is quite possible to mine gold or to polish a diamond; but these must be there in the first place. The bulk of the young workers coming up into industry must, in the nature of things, remain routine workers.

But the abilities possessed by routine people, even though they be less than superior, may yet be of a very high order. Nor would it be desirable either for industry or for society did not Nature provide this difference in inherent capacity, so that some people are best fitted to do the simpler types of work and others to carry on the more complex, the more difficult, and the more highly organized labors. It is thus that all the work of the world, the ordinary and the unusual, gets itself accomplished. Difficulty in industry is created not by this natural difference in aptitudes, but by the tendency to look down on all workers who do not get into executive positions, to consider them failures, instead of appreciating the importance of the work they do in their own place. If a woman's capacities fit her to be a routine worker, she is doing her part to keep the wheels of industry moving provided she is as good a one as she can possibly train herself to be.

Because younger people come into the modern complex industrial system with a training far more diversified than that of their forerunners, are the routine workers of the "old school" thereby rendered useless to industry? Do only young workers trained under our more extended educational régime fit into modern business organization?

That is most doubtful. Young workers, since they begin their industrial career in an age replete with advances in science, have the advantage of enjoying many mechanical comforts and conveniences, and have access to many educational resources, that were absent from the youth of their forebears in industry. It is a mad, whirling age. Speed, snap, pep are the watchwords of the moment. The end to which all this hurry leads is not easy for the philosophically inclined to discern. Yet when airplanes cast aside thousands of miles as naught, when automobiles and trains whiz past in a flash, when radio transmission of sounds and of photographs is a matter of seconds, these breathtaking scientific and commercial developments sting every one's blood. Older women and young workers are alike quickened by them.

But there is another side to the shield. It is an age, too, where application, patience and thoroughness seem superfluous. For scarcely is a thing perfected and recognized when another, perhaps not as good, but new at any rate, takes its place—a condition general in industry. The habit of doing things for the moment seems but a logical result of these swift industrial variations. Then, too, the less conscientiously run newspapers and the "tabloids" often deliberately misspell ordinary words in feature advertisements and in comic scrips, ingraining these errors through constant repetition, and thus defeat the aim of the schools to teach correct spelling. Machines that do their calculating for them take from these routine workers the mental exercise of calculating for themselves. While the gain in speed from the use of these machines is desirable for industry, it cannot be denied that they make for less mental agility on the part of employees who use them.

Therefore, in balancing the capabilities of the young routine worker of to-day against those of the older woman who is the product of an earlier but more thorough system, little seems to be found in the superior training of the former to justify the barring of the latter from the field of modern industry.

Yes, in this drama of the middle-aged woman in industry her part is just now far from a stellar one. It is not desired that she be given such a part regardless of her ability to fill it. It is only asked that she be given an opportunity to try out for it, on an equal footing with all others who have her training and experience—that she be allowed to enter the competition without handicaps. The rest is in her own hands.

CHAPTER II

THE EMPLOYER'S POINT OF VIEW

I

THE motivating force back of all policies governing the hiring and firing of older women is the attitude of the employer himself. He may express his ideas through newspaper advertisements, through agencies, or through managers. But it is he who formulates them. And he is generally actuated in any decisions he may make regarding such employees by what he thinks will yield him the highest net return.

These employers may be huge corporations made up of several units, each of which was, before its incorporation into the larger group, a very considerable organization on its own account. They may be single small-scale corporations. They may be engaged in some form of public or personal service. They may be organizations devoted to making and marketing goods for the everyday use of the consuming public. Whatever their size or the nature of their business, they are all interested in procuring as much capital as possible in order still further to increase and ramify their plants.

To enable them to do this the public must buy their stocks. The public will do so only when it is assured that such securities will yield them sufficiently large dividends. These dividends will increase in size for the stock-holders with every decrease in operating expenses. Wages form a considerable slice of the variable expenses in any plant. It is obviously desirable for any concern to keep its payroll at the lowest possible level consistent with the greatest standard output of which it is capable.

When we consider these things it is not surprising that it is especially the large-scale corporations who are foremost in establishing maximum age limits, and fixing these limits below the line of demarcation for middle age; for the wages that young employees are willing to accept are low because their inexperience commands only a low sum in the labor market. The difference between what they will take and what a full-fledged worker in the field would demand is the price young workers pay for catching up in technical mastery with the latter. Besides, the great majority of young workers live with their parents or other relatives. While in many cases they must contribute to the family fund, the amount is usually considerably less than what they would have to pay for board, lodging and clothing were they living alone. Therefore, their expenses being less, they can manage to subsist on a lower wage than can thoroughly experienced workers who must support themselves and perhaps others.

So the young workers are hired. Their salaries as they appear on the payroll are small. But their salaries are not the only items of expense to the concern. In New York State the Workmen's Compensation Law makes it obligatory on practically every industry in it to insure its employees against accident. The rates for such insurance increase where the nature of the business involves much hazard and with the size of the payroll. Older women too are considered more liable to accidents; more accidents and their higher salaries swell the rates. Besides, most firms carry for their employees group insurance covering both health and life. Rates for the former increase with the proportion of women employed. For the latter they rise in direct ratio with the increasing age of the employees.

These facts are often given by large-scale corporations as reasons why they establish the age limits that practically shut older women out of their employ. But are they valid? In group health-insurance, for instance, the rates are higher for women than they are for men, as shown in Figure XII. Presumably these higher rates exist because women are considered to be more liable to accidents and illnesses. But there is strong evidence to the contrary.

The Women's Bureau of the New York State Department of Labor issued in June, 1926, a special bulletin on "Some Recent Figures on Accidents to Women and Minors." In the course of it the following statement is made: "During the entire period from 1917 to 1925 the proportion of accidents to females never rose above seven per cent."* In analyzing this seven per cent for the year ending June

* Page 7.

FIGURE XII

MONTHLY RATES PER $1.00 WEEKLY INDEMNITY FOR STANDARD GROUPS
AETNA LIFE INSURANCE CO.

	Less than 11% female employees	11%-21% fem. emp.	21%-31% fem. emp.	31%-41% fem. emp.	41%-51% fem. emp.	51%-61% fem. emp.	61%-71% fem. emp.	71%-81% fem. emp.	81%-91% fem. emp.	91%-100% fem. emp.
Plan 2	.083	.096	.104	.113	.121	.129	.138	.146	.154	.163
2A	.100	.115	.125	.135	.145	.155	.165	.175	.185	.195
2B	.113	.129	.141	.152	.163	.174	.186	.197	.208	.219
3	.070	.080	.087	.094	.101	.108	.115	.122	.129	.136
3A	.086	.099	.107	.116	.124	.133	.141	.150	.159	.167
3B	.098	.113	.123	.132	.142	.152	.162	.172	.182	.191
4	.053	.061	.066	.072	.077	.082	.087	.093	.098	.103
4A	.068	.078	.084	.091	.098	.105	.112	.118	.125	.132
4B	.080	.092	.099	.107	.115	.123	.131	.139	.147	.155
5	.073	.084	.091	.098	.106	.113	.120	.128	.135	.142
5A	.090	.103	.112	.121	.130	.139	.148	.157	.166	.175
5B	.103	.118	.128	.138	.149	.159	.169	.179	.190	.200

These rates provide illness and non-occupational accident coverage for periods varying from thirteen through fifty-two weeks.

30, 1925, we find that, of all the accidents happening to women in industry, fifty-six per cent occurred in the manufacturing field, thirty-three per cent in clerical and personal service, and nine per cent in trade, which includes selling. Of the women in manufacturing, 76.7 per cent of the women between eighteen and twenty years old met with accidents, but only 49.6 per cent of those over twenty-one years of age were injured. In clerical and personal service work and in trade, however, the reverse is the case. Only 15.7 per cent of the clerical workers between eighteen and twenty years old, but 38.3 per cent of those over twenty-one years old, were compensated for accidents in that year. In trade the difference is not so great—6.6 per cent for the group between eighteen and twenty years old as compared with nine per cent for all those over twenty-one years of age.

However, it must be remembered in judging these figures that the eighteen to twenty year group covers only three working years, while those in the group over twenty years old covers the entire range of years beginning at the first year of legal majority and extending over the age of the oldest employees at work in any of these industries. In the absence of definite statistics on that point any statement as to the greatest frequency group for accidents to those over twenty years old must be mere conjecture. But on the basis of the size of the figures for the eighteen to twenty year groups, may we not be justified in assuming that most of the accidents in the twenty-one year plus group would, on investigation, prove to be in the earlier years of the schedule?

Whether or not this be true, it is certain that women, according to this report, meet with only a very small percentage of accidents at any age or in any industry, in spite of the fact that women form twenty-five per cent of the working population of the State. This makes it hard to understand why most insurance companies charge more for insuring women against accident or illness than they do for similar insurance for men.

An article appearing in *The World* for October 9, 1927, may furnish a clew to the situation. The companies quoted in this article state that women are inclined to stop work and report themselves as "disabled" more frequently than are men. That, they think, is because, since single women generally live at home and married women can turn to their husbands if they must, they suffer less from the consequences of losing time than would men who must care for families and who would on this account try to lose as little work time as possible. Whether or not this is so generally true as to justify an increase of twenty to twenty-five per cent in insurance rates to firms where many women are employed is a matter that firms who must pay this increase might do well to consider. As far as accidents to women per se are concerned, the State report quoted seems to offer support for the suggestion that, if any revision in rates for women be undertaken, they might take a downward rather than an upward trend.

Since these rates are based on sex and not on age, their existence can hardly be charged exclusively to the older women in industry. Although most companies increase the rates somewhat when there is an unusually large number of women at the older ages on the payroll of any concern, these rates are, on the whole, part of the inevitable expenses of operating a business the carrying on of which requires the employment of many women, whatever their ages may be.

II

The second element in the group insurance situation so often given by employers as a reason for not hiring older women is the fact that the rates increase with the age of the employee, so that hiring older women automatically becomes more expensive.

Such rising rates are usually a feature of the type of policy that provides for the payment of a maximum sum to the family of an employee whose death occurs while he is at his employment. These policies closely resemble ordinary life insurance policies, the chief differences being, first, the fact that the employer, not the worker, takes out the insurance; and secondly, that the liability of the company in case of the death of an employee is usually limited to $5,000. Most concerns employing many women carry simultaneously both the first and the second types of group insurance—that is, the type of group insurance that protects the employer against accident and disability claims on the part of employees, the rates for which he must cover whenever he hires women of any age in any number, and the type that covers and limits his liability in case the employee dies while in his employ.

Let us see how great is the increase in rates on the second type of policy, so often given in employment offices to defend the erection of age barriers. The accompanying schedule shows the premium rates for risk at the minimum, which includes occupations and business concerns such as we have been considering throughout this study—banks, mail order houses, insurance companies, retail stores, and "industries where there is no occupational or other store hazard."

In examining these rates, it must be borne in mind that the policies they represent cover death benefits to the families of employees, and that therefore the nature of the work these policies do in itself raises the insurance rates. Yet the difference in the monthly rate between that for employees of twenty-five and the rate for those of thirty-five is only four cents; and that between the rates for twenty-five and for forty-five years of age only thirty-two cents per month. Assuming that a concern employs 500 women, if they have applications from women up to and including thirty-five years old, but if they draw age lines at twenty-five years of age, they save by this process a sum somewhere between $270, which is the aggregate monthly premium for age twenty-five, and $290, the aggregate monthly premium for age thirty-five. This is twenty dollars a month for a la-

FIGURE XIII

MINIMUM MONTHLY PREMIUMS FOR $1,000 OF
INSURANCE

EQUITABLE LIFE ASSURANCE CO.

Attained Age of Employee	Successive Monthly Premiums	Attained Age of Employee	Successive Monthly Premiums
15	.47	38	.63
16	.47	39	.65
17	.48	40	.67
18	.48	41	.70
19	.49	42	.74
20	.50	43	.77
21	.51	44	.81
22	.52	45	.86
23	.53	46	.91
24	.53	47	.97
25	.54	48	1.03
26	.54	49	1.11
27	.55	50	1.18
28	.55	51	1.27
29	.55	52	1.36
30	.55	53	1.47
31	.55	54	1.58
32	.56	55	1.71
33	.56	56	1.84
34	.57	57	1.99
35	.58	58	2.15
36	.59	59	2.33
37	.61	60	2.52

bor force of 500 women. For a whole year this is, in round numbers, $240. The sum will not be quite so large because, if these payments are made for the twelve months at one time and in advance, a four per cent discount will be allowed by the insurance company. Furthermore, not all of these employees will be thirty-five years old; many will be less.

If we take the difference between the aggregate monthly premium of $270 for the twenty-five year old workers and that for the forty-five year old employees, or $430, we have a monthly difference of $160, or a yearly difference of $1,920 for 500 workers, assuming, which is highly improbable, that all 500 women are at or near the forty-five year limit. Calculations anywhere along the line will reveal similarly small possible savings.

Most large-scale employers, as has before been pointed out, not only insure themselves against death claims through policies of this kind, but also turn over to insurance companies, for premium considerations, the matter of paying their workers sick benefits. Turning for a moment to Figure XII, we find, assuming that the women employed in the plant we are considering number sixty per cent of the total payroll of the concern, that for a thirteen week benefit the rate is $.129 a month for each dollar to be paid per week. In other words, if the worker's weekly salary is $18 and the indemnity to be paid, as is usually the case, amounts to two-thirds of this, or $12, the monthly premium paid by the firm for turning this possible payment over to the insurance company is $1.548, or $18.576 for a whole year. If the plant we are considering employs 500 women at forty-five years of age, the total amount this plant can possibly pay for turning over to an insurance company all its death and total disability liability, plus its minimum illness liability for this entire force of older women for a whole year, exclusive of Workmen's Compensation rates, is $9,288 for the illness benefit and $5,160 for a year's life insurance, or a total of $14,448 for both. If the labor force were only twenty-five years old in a plant employing 500 women of which these made up sixty per cent of the payroll, the $9,288 would remain unchanged; but the life insurance and total disability premium for a year would be only $3,240. This would make the total group insurance bill for this concern $12,528, or a total saving, as has before been demonstrated, of only $1,920. This is the sum for the sake of which, for a force of 500 women, concerns say that they will not hire older workers. It is a sum larger than the reality because not all the 500 women considered will be forty-five years old. But it must be remembered that most companies charge more where there are many older women; so that this fact may be considered to balance the age rate discrepancy just mentioned.

III

Employers who give higher group insurance rates as their reason for barring older women from their plants usually couple with it the additional statement that such workers are also greater pension risks. Is the latter reason any more tenable than the former?

In most concerns pensions become operative only after a certain set period of service. How, then, can older women obtain them any faster than young workers unless they, too, have given this definite number of years to the firm? A woman is a pensioned employee whether she retire after thirty-five years of service at fifty-five or at sixty-five years of age. Since it is hardly the policy of well-established concerns continuing under approximately the same management to get rid of their old employees before they reach pensioning age, young workers, as well as those that are older when hired, will, after serving for the same length of time, ultimately reach the goal of retirement on a pension. The only possible danger of increased pension eligibility from older workers would appear if a certain age limit regardless of the number of years of service were made the retirement age—a system that, as far as we know, is nowhere in existence.

Nor has it been established that older women are more inclined to be absent from duty because of illness than are young workers, thereby oftener becoming claimants for sick benefits. On the contrary, most of the employers interviewed—even those who did not look with especial favor on the hiring of older women—gave them credit for decided regularity and faithfulness on the job. In such circumstances it appears safe to conclude that the possibility of pension and sick benefit savings may be eliminated as sound reasons that actuate employers in hiring younger rather than older workers.

IV

Investigations conducted by the Bureau of Women in Industry of the New York State Department of Labor* put the median wage for mercantile workers in New York City at $18.25 a week for full-time work. In some of the firms visited for this study the weekly wages were as follows:

Unskilled Mercantile	$16
Cafeteria, full time	15, 16
Cafeteria, part time	7
Clerical Work	18 to 25
Candy Factory	18 to 20
Pattern Folding (seasonal):	
piece work	20 to 30
weekly wages	15
inexperienced	12
Domestic (including room and meals)	12.50 to 20

As a rule, the lower schedules represent the wages paid to the younger workers while the higher are the pay of the more experienced. Taking the median found by official survey as our standard, let us measure by means of an example, as we can to some extent, the difference in the size of the payrolls that the hiring of young workers brings about.

In selling, for instance, the beginner receives $15 or $16. The difference between this wage and the

* "Hours and Earnings of Women in Five Industries." New York State Department of Labor, Nov., 1923, p. 78.

median is $2.25 a week, or $117 for a year of full time work. The highly experienced workers, chiefly older women, receive approximately $25, which is an increase of $6.75 a week, or $351 per full time year, over the median. Let us assume that in a department store employing 1,000 saleswomen a policy of age limit fixation is decided on. In this shop the older women hired formerly covered twenty-five per cent of the sales force. Their average salary was $25 a week, which made the aggregate salaries paid to all their older salespeople, 250 in number, $6,250 a week. Of the other seventy-five per cent, two-thirds, or fifty per cent of the total force, received the median wage, or $18.25. Thus the total weekly payroll for these 500 workers was $9,125. The remaining twenty-five per cent were the young workers at the minimum wage of $15. The total weekly expense for their services was $3,750. The median and the minimum wage workers together received $12,875. In other words, seventy-five per cent of the force could be hired at a little more than twice as much as the amount that must be paid to the twenty-five per cent at the top of the payroll. It is decided to put up age barriers and to take as new workers only those willing to accept the median salary. The upper twenty-five per cent will now ask for $4,562.50 instead of $6,250. The firm does not hire totally inexperienced workers, nor yet the most expert it can obtain. It saves on the salaries of these 250 workers a total of $1,687.50 a week, or $87,750 a year.

This may look like a large sum. Yet large department stores easily spend the amount saved in this way in a whole week on one single day's advertising. Of the many thousands of customers that come in response to advertisements, if only a few are served less efficiently than they might be, the resultant loss easily nullifies this saving in salaries. It is not the absolute amount saved, but the amount in relation to what its expenditure might have brought the firm, that really counts.

Examples might easily enough be cited to show that correspondence carried on less efficiently than it might be, factory work entailing the wasting of time and materials because poorer workers are hired than might have been obtained, mean a greater loss in the long run than the savings effected in the salaries paid to less expert workers. In industry as well as everywhere else, the best obtainable is often the cheapest in the end. The results obtained from the hiring of older and more experienced workers as contrasted with those attained by less expert employees are not so intangible that they cannot be figured out, to an approximate extent at least, by interested employers. Their own interests would be served were they to do so.

V

The most expensive element in the make-up of a payroll is not the higher salaries that the best workers are paid, but the intangible, though none the less

present, cost of changing workers on a given job—
the labor turnover. In an attempt to estimate this
with some accuracy for the particular concerns we
have been studying, the astonishing situation was
revealed, in response to inquiries, that even the largest concerns considered kept no record of their turnover either by age or by length of service. One shop
supplied data grouping their present staff by ages
and length of service; but information regarding the
turnover during the year for which these employment statistics were given can only be inferred indi-
rectly through a study of the material supplied. The
superintendent of another firm, by the fact that he
referred the inquirer to the State Bureau of Housing
for the information sought, made the investigator
wonder whether he quite understood the nature of
the material about which inquiry was made.

Yet this matter of turnover forms a leak that cannot spell other than financial loss to the concern affected. Much study has been made on the subject of
turnover; but none, as far as is discoverable, on the
situation as it exists in the many large plants in New
York City, either generally or by sex and age groups.

The shop whose employment statistics were previously mentioned supplied the data used in Figure
XIV.

As will be seen from this chart, out of a total labor
force of 1,717 women, 619 are over thirty-five years
of age. Since the number of workers serving the firm
five years or longer is 576, this figure, which is very

FIGURE XIV

FEMALE LABOR FORCE, JAN.–DEC., 1927

Occupations	Below 21 years old	21–34	35–44	45+
Saleswomen.....	85	198	132	85
Clerical.........	263	309	195	75
Other...........	108	135	78	54
Totals........	456	642	405	214

SERVICE LENGTH, FEMALE LABOR FORCE, JAN.–DEC., 1927

Less than three months..................	40
3–6 months............................	83
6 months–1 year........................	122
1–5 years.............................	896
5 years+..............................	576
Total.............................	1,717

close to the group of 619 for the total of older women, probably substantiates fairly well the contention that older employees are not likely to change
positions easily. A little larger numerically than this
group of older women is the group between the ages
of twenty-one to thirty-four years—a total of 642
workers. Probably the bulk of these form the major
part of the 896 workers who have been with this concern for periods varying from one to five years. From

the group less than twenty-one years old, or 456 workers, we may probably deduct most of those who served the concern for periods varying from less than three months to a year—245 workers in all. The difference of 211 workers probably makes up most of the balance needed to complete the group serving from one to five years.

In this particular concern the turnover appears to be particularly light, as far as we can judge from the data at our disposal. The 245 workers who have served it less than a year form only 14.2 per cent of the total force employed by it. Any attempt to decide whether most of this percentage falls in the selling or in the clerical group must be mere conjecture. But in order to arrive at some idea of the monetary charge on a concern even where the turnover rate is as small as it appears to be here, let us assume that in this group there has been only one separation from each position during the given year—an assumption that, if we are to judge by turnover records generally, is probably much below the actual situation. Let us assume further that all the separations were among the clerical workers. At the rate of $29 each* (which is the expense incurred in the process of each separation), the total amount lost by this concern in one year from this source alone was $7,105 —which is probably much less than the actuality.

Employment managers in practically all the plants

* "The Turnover of Labor." Federal Board for Vocational Education, Washington, D. C., 1919.

visited for this study concurred in saying that the turnover among young workers for their particular concern was considerable. They also agreed that among older workers this situation was practically absent. The reasons for the difference in staying qualities in the two age groups were indicated in a general way in a brief article appearing in the January, 1919, number of *Industrial Management*. The author diagnoses the difficulty as a vague feeling among young workers that they "do not like to work there." They arrive at this conclusion because:

1. They have been taught that they have a right to be happy.

2. They desire to do something worth while.

3. They expect appreciation.

Where these things are either lacking or insufficient, the young workers "do not like to work there"; and so leave. Older women, however, have become resigned to doing without these things; and so they are more likely to make the best of such positions as they can find.

Some interesting schedules of turnover percentages* concern the records of fifty-three establishments, including manufacturing plants and public utilities corporations, in which the percentage of workers who had held their positions for less than a year amounted to forty per cent of the total number of workers in them. The cost of each separation in a manufacturing plant is variously estimated as from

* "Labor Turnover in Industry."   Dr. P. F. Brissenden, 1922.

$20 to $81 per worker.* In a plant large enough, for instance, to involve 2,000 workers in these separations in a given year, the total cost from labor turnover alone would range from $40,000 to $162,000 per year.

The cost of turnover is an individual matter in each concern; for the amount of it necessarily varies with seasonality, with hazard, with the type and condition of the work itself, and with the quality of the supervision exercised. But whatever the amount involved, there must necessarily be some loss to the firm in material wasted, in wear and tear on machinery, and in expert work time lost in breaking in new workers. Where the work does not require the handling of raw materials or machinery there are other routine matters to take their place that in the aggregate also mean loss to the concerns that encounter the turnover.

It would appear, therefore, that it would be well worth the time of a firm's cost accountant to go deeply into this matter of labor turnover, especially with respect to a comparison of its frequency among young as contrasted with older workers. A form like that on the following page might prove useful.

After these figures on turnover were obtained, further research by the cost accountant might unearth interesting information relative to turnover costs among young workers as compared with the higher

* "The Turnover of Labor." Federal Board for Vocational Education, Washington, D. C., 1919.

FIGURE XV

FORM FOR COMPUTING TURNOVER COSTS

FEMALE LABOR TURNOVER

Occupation	Below 21 years old	21-34	35-44	45+	Average cost of turnover per person
Saleswomen............					
Clerical...............					
Other................					
SERVICE					
Less than 3 months....					
3–6 months...........					
6 months–1 year.......					
1–5 years............					
5 years..............					

The total female labor force is ....

group insurance rates necessary to protect steady older women; differences in the salaries paid to older as compared with younger workers for the same type of work; and differences in output between the average of the young worker and that of the expert older woman. It is doubtful whether many firms would find, even though the older woman's services seemed on the surface to cost more, that the tabulations did not show the older woman's output to have more than balanced the slightly higher cost of keeping her on the payroll.

VI

Since, then, group insurance rates, higher salaries, and greater pension liability may be discounted as strong arguments weighing against the employment of older women, why are older women so often denied places in industry? Probably the strongest reason is a psychological rather than a practical one. Many young men have risen to places of responsibility in industry, some by sheer ability, others by the aid of fortuitous circumstances. Here and there the older women with whom they have come in contact may have had undesirable personal traits. More frequently older people of acknowledged skill in subordinate places no doubt made uncomfortable their young superiors who, perhaps less able than they, were nevertheless compelled through the exigencies of organization to give them orders; and sometimes these older people were tactless enough to let their young superiors know that they resented orders coming from them. All these things have combined to give the older woman a reputation for inadaptability, cantankerousness, and lack of enthusiasm; and so an injurious composite picture of the older woman in industry has got abroad in the land, and has, in the manner of type ideas, imbedded itself in the public consciousness.

But is the older woman always alone in being a bit cantankerous? Did not a few of the interviews previously described here indicate that an occasional employment manager, too, had allowed his point of view to become a trifle jaundiced, as far as the older woman was concerned? For even if individuals among these older women are poor material, is not that the case, too, among young people? Are not the rank and file of young routine workers to-day much the same type as those of yesterday? Glance at the groups of these young women in the subway trains. Undoubtedly they have youthful strength and enthusiasm. But would these necessarily be devoted to the work in hand? Besides, is "pep" a universal youthful characteristic? Are there not among young people languid, indifferent, even sour, individuals? Are not many of these present-day young people also of the type that will let the years of their youth slip by them, enjoying them and their small salaries as they come, without a thought of the future—the middle-aged problem people of to-morrow? Did not some of them, young as they are, shut the door of their mental development firmly behind them with their last day of compulsory schooling? Yet many times these are the types of young people preferred to older women who, if they are not more highly developed personally, at least can bring to employers the benefit of training and experience. As an editorial in the New York *Times* of October 12, 1927, discussing "Work for the Middle-aged," has it:

"The wise employer will know how to mobilize his young men for first-line service and the older men for the less strenuous but equally important duties of the second line and behind the lines. Germany came very near winning the World War and succeeded in prolonging it beyond expectations by precisely such use of her middle-aged reserves."

That is as true of older women as of middle-aged men.

Employers who interview older women applying for positions may be a little dismayed because these women look anxious instead of gay and hopeful. They are worried; and under such circumstances they do not look their best. Even those who now hold positions are somewhat uneasy where, as in one concern that was previously mentioned, the attitude of the employer is known to be unfavorable to them. With the cloud of imminent unemployment hovering over them, is it any wonder they cannot always produce their best output?

It would be well for them, before this cloud develops into a storm, if they could be made to see the reasons for their possible exposure to it. But would the employer then lose nothing? Is it not quite possible that with the passing of the present middle-aged incumbents in a concern, the species may become extinct? For, with large turnovers among young workers everywhere admitted, whence are to come our future old employees? The employer will then have little opportunity to gaze long upon the same countenances; and after a time even variety may become monotonous.

Be that as it may, the erection of age barriers at the door of any concern makes the efforts of older women to be self-supporting so much harder. But it may, too, keep from the firm loyal, worth-while employees. Perhaps never before in industry has mutual understanding been so necessary, or the results from the lack of it so full of the promise of suffering.

Women are comparatively new in industry, and so their problems are not yet very old. This one—this question of the desirability of employing older women—is just looming on the horizon. Must it grow to the proportions that it has already assumed for men?

CHAPTER III

THE STATE AND THE PROBLEM

I

ADJUSTING industrial tangles through legislative means is probably the swiftest and at the same time the most generally equable and comprehensive method of solving these problems that has yet been devised. Employers and workers both are so differently developed temperamentally, educationally, and technically that, left to themselves, nothing generally beneficial would ever be accomplished, although some good things would undoubtedly be done in specific instances. But State legislation can draw the broadly important features out of the mass of detail that surrounds any question of social importance. It can, with one sweep of its powerful arm, clear away the hindrances that render any group of industrial workers less efficient than they might otherwise be.

Certain conditions in industry hamper the commercial progress of the older woman. They exist, not because they were malevolently put there to block her path, but because, since she is a comparatively new entrant into industry, her problems have not yet been extensively investigated or discussed. A study of her problems and an interest in them have now become necessary in order that she may have her opportunity to function freely as an economic agent. Changed social conditions have decreed her entrance into the business world. Somehow she must find support. It is far better for the entire social fabric if she herself be the one to pay her own way; and in the great majority of cases she is very anxious to do so.

The following paragraphs indicate a few of the ways in which the State could help her to attain self-support. In the eddy of modern industry, with its constantly shifting currents, new entrants may easily be a bit bewildered in trying to reach their destination of economic stability. The industries that must absorb them may not quite understand either how to go about it, or what would be gained by taking them in. The State, which has at heart the interest of both workers and employers, is frequently the only agent that can secure the greatest good to both through wise laws. Perhaps the following may contain some suggestions toward that end.

II

When the New York State Workmen's Compensation Law went into effect in 1913 it was hailed as a splendid piece of constructive legislation, which indeed it was. Protection against industrial accidents and illnesses for workers was a long step forward not only in guarding their person, but also in bringing about more efficient work on their part through the elimination of one source of worry—the care of dependents should they be hurt while at their employments.

It has, on the whole, worked out quite as well as was expected. The last thing in the minds of its framers was probably the conception that, beneficial as it generally was, it might in any way work injury to any group of employees. Yet, according to the statements of some of the employment managers interviewed for this study, that is in effect just what has happened.

For older and more experienced workers usually get higher salaries; they are also considered greater accident risks; these things raise the rates. Besides, group insurance rates are higher, first, for women as women, secondly, for older women. These facts have become strong elements opposing the employment of older women in business.

Can it be demonstrated that, industry for industry, older women in commercial life are more liable to illness or to accident than are younger women? Theoretically it may seem logical. But actually the New York State Labor Department report heretofore quoted lends only negative support to such an argument; and the statements of employment managers generally that older women attend regularly are testimony in refutation of it. Only by means of an extensive, state-wide survey undertaken by government authority through an organization like the

Bureau of Women in Industry of the New York State Department of Labor, or under the direction of the Women's Bureau of the United States Department of Labor, can it ever be established just what the situation really is regarding the tendency of older women to apply for disability allowances. These organizations, by analyzing material as to the relative claims of each age group on the welfare funds of the different establishments, could bring out some valuable information on this point. The findings established could be used in two ways. First, insurance companies could use them as a basis for a revision of group insurance rates upward or downward insofar as the results of the investigation showed such revision to be just and necessary. Secondly, if no adequate reason were found to account for the higher rates for older women, and in the highly improbable event that the insurance companies were to refuse to revise their rates voluntarily, they could be asked to do so under the State Insurance Law.

Let us assume that there were found to be more illnesses and accidents among older than among younger workers. The New York State report on accidents to women and minors from which we have before quoted, gives the accident rates for women of all ages in the State as approximately only seven per cent of all industrial accidents occurring in it. Even if the bulk of these were among the older women employees, the percentage is still so very small that higher rates for them do not appear to be justified in the circumstances. Not only this point but also the fact that establishments employing large numbers of women must pay extra rates, appear to need elucidation on the part of the insurance companies. The State would confer a real benefit on its older women workers as well as on the industries that employ them were the insurance companies asked to take up this whole matter for possible revision of their rates. If that were done, and the rates changed in favor of the older women, one strong prop now used to support the tendency to avoid employing them would fall away; and the older woman's problems would be simplified to that extent.

III

The New York State Department of Labor maintains among other excellent sub-divisions a Bureau of Statistics and Information, a Women's Bureau, and a State Employment Agency. The first two are fairly well co-ordinated. What is urgently needed is some method of procedure that will bring the State Employment Agency in closer touch with these two.

If all three of these departments were to work as a unit, much good for the older woman in industry as well as for all women must inevitably follow. Results of investigations into labor conditions in any given industry made by the Women's Bureau could be used by the employment bureau to build up connections, to transmit information to applicants, or to move labor units, as the circumstances might require. Statistical information analyzed and tabulated by the Bureau of Research could be made the basis of study by the employment bureau as to possible work opportunities. Information gained from workers who apply for help, on the one hand, and employers who ask for help, on the other, might be used by the Women's Bureau as starting-points of investigation and study in fields helpful to women, information about which is not yet adequate.

Especially is such co-ordination necessary for material concerning the older woman, if her position in the future is to be made more tenable than it now appears to be. The many angles in the problem of her industrial efficiency and the tenure of her employment are fields at present practically untouched. Information regarding her training and business qualifications, her points of superiority and her weak points, her chances of obtaining work in the different industries, figures concerning absence and turnover among them, and many other points of importance concerning her, await investigation and tabulation. The older woman will no doubt seek means of self-support in the future even more extensively than she is now doing. Therefore if she is to function at her best, more must be known about her and about the conditions governing her chances for finding employment than is at present the case. The machinery provided by the State, would it but turn its powers in her direction, could do much to help her solve her problems.

IV

Private employment agencies play so large a part at the present time in making labor adjustments that anything tending to raise their general level must result in bettering placement conditions throughout the State. Some of them are at present operated by intelligent, well qualified people; but too many are headed by owners who, however well-intentioned they may be, lack both the intelligence and the training to realize the tremendous possibilities inherent in their work.

It is easy enough to recognize the importance of work that aims, on the one hand, to find places where workers may give their time to successful functioning, and, on the other, to provide centres where industry may obtain the most efficient possible assistance. Yet this serious matter is now left to haphazard adjustments, with consequently poor results at both ends.

The State has in its hands the possibility of relieving this situation to a great extent. It has long since recognized that standards for any kind of work that affects the physical, the educational, or the economic welfare of its citizens must be set up and maintained. To this end it has established a State University, which administers its work through the

State Board of Regents. State standards are set up and State examinations are given for the physicians, the lawyers, the teachers, the dentists, and the accountants that are allowed to practise within its borders. Such examinations include, as a rule, not only tests of the applicant's training and education, but also, as far as this can be provided, certification as to character.

Personnel work is a highly complex vocation. Rightly developed it might reasonably attain to the rank of a profession. For in order to understand the worker's present capacities and shortcomings, and in order to be able to bring out his latent possibilities, training very similar to the background in psychology possessed by the teacher or the physician is necessary. A thorough knowledge of economic theory as well as practical work in business organization, finance and banking are required in order to understand the employer's end of the labor adjustment problem. These are but special fields that might form part of a generally sound educational background. A fine, sympathetic personality as the motivating power back of this technical equipment is essential for success.

These are professional requirements. But the work of placing employees is important enough to rank with that of caring for the teeth or for a firm's accounts. The State Board of Regents could give examinations to those desiring to conduct employment agencies, and license only successful candidates. Not only would this step result in the elimination of incompetent bureaus, but it would raise the whole level of personnel work.

This improvement would inevitably be felt in personnel offices everywhere throughout the State. For those who now occupy positions in department stores, factories, and particularly in giant corporations could, too, be required to obtain a certificate showing their fitness for carrying on their work. Many of the clerks who now do preliminary interviewing in personnel offices would immediately be disqualified. Their replacement by competent workers would be a boon to older women. For it is inconceivable that men and women intelligent enough to pass rigid tests for so serious an occupation as personnel work would be capable of conducting their offices on any other basis than that of filling any given position with the best qualified worker, old or young, that could be obtained.

V

It is sometimes suggested that the State operate an employment bureau especially designed for older workers, both men and women. Since the work that can be done by the two sexes often differs widely, the present plan of the State Employment Agency of operating separate departments for men and for women would probably prove an excellent way in which to conduct such an agency for older workers.

To be successful a specialized agency of this nature would need to do special contact work among interested firms, and missionary work among concerns inclined to regard the matter with indifference or opposition. It would need to know first the fields in which the older workers were having the most employment difficulty, and the reasons therefor. It would need to be prepared with convincing arguments and material to present to employers, that these might feel confident that no financial loss to them would result if they hired older people. It would need to do very careful work in grouping and classifying the applicants not only by type of work requested, but by degrees of efficiency in handling the kinds of work they wanted. The applicant's word for what she could do would not necessarily need to be accepted in such a State agency. Co-operation with the continuation, the vocational, and the commercial schools of the State could no doubt be brought about whereby these applicants could be subjected to a practical test and graded according to its findings. Applicants sent out from a State Bureau after such classification would carry with them the backing of authoritative knowledge as to what they could really do; and this fact could not fail to impress the employer. Defects brought to light by such examination could be pointed out to the applicant, together with suggestions for eliminating them either by further training at some school or else by personal determination and will power, according to their nature. The possibilities of such a bureau for helping older women are obvious.

Such an agency would need expert guidance; and experts in any field are expensive to engage. However, the entire cost of obtaining them for this work need not necessarily devolve on the State. The agency could be made practically self-supporting by charging the applicant a fee graduated according to the amount and character of the service rendered to her, making also a charge for its service to the employer. Both sides would willingly pay for help of this kind; it would not burden the taxpayers; and all industry would benefit by its establishment.

VI

On November 9, 1927, there appeared in the New York *Sun* an inconspicuous news item headed:

COLLAPSES OF HUNGER
Former Salesman, 64, Found Starving in Street.

"***, 64 years old," the article continues, "formerly head drapery salesman over a period of twenty years for one of the city's largest department stores, was taken to *** Hospital last night when police of the *** Station found he was too weak to eat the food they had bought for him after he had been brought in from the street, where he had collapsed from hunger."

The story of the discovery of the man follows. Then it ends:

"*** told the police he lost his position as head drapery salesman at the department store because of advancing age three years ago. The officials of this store have been notified of the old man's condition."

Quite evidently this particular shop had no pension system for its employees. It will be recalled that some of the managers visited for this study admitted that there was no such system in their particular establishment. Just how wide-spread this lack of a pension system is among business concerns is another field in which the State could legitimately take an interest.

In the particular instance covered by the news item quoted the employee himself may have been at fault for not having saved enough for his old age. On the other hand, his salary may always have been so low and his financial obligations so great that such provision for himself was practically impossible. It does not matter who was specifically at fault in this instance. But the fact that an employee may be discharged when old age comes on, without any provision for him after twenty years of service, does matter very much.

Would it not be possible for the State to enact legislation that would make a pension system automatic in any concern employing, let us say, five or more persons? Furthermore, could not the employees themselves provide most of the capital for it? Could they not deposit with their firms for this purpose a small portion of their earnings every week, these savings to start with their first week's salary? The accumulated fund could be invested through insurance companies or other agencies authorized to undertake this work. Each employee's account could be credited with the amount of these accruals, which could be withdrawn at any time the employees severed their connection with the concern before reaching retiring age. But if they remained until they were eligible for retirement, these accruals plus the accumulated compound interest they earned could be converted into an annuity, payable to them for the rest of their lives.

The New York *Times* of September 11, 1927, carries an article in the course of which pensioning systems are described. Some of these systems, most of which were inaugurated by large scale corporations, make such annuities rewards for faithful service, usually varying from fifteen to thirty years in length. Other corporations have systems whereby the employees themselves pay out of wages the monthly premiums that later give them their annuities, on the same principle according to which life insurance endowment policies are a system of compulsory saving. This is generally speaking the preferable of the two plans.

Legislation enacted by the State to inaugurate a pension system as a matter of routine in mercantile

and manufacturing plants would do away with trage-
dies such as the one described in the news item we
have quoted. It would give the worker, especially the
routine employee, a feeling of security that would
go far toward removing the depression so often objected to in older workers, because the anxiety about
old age provision that so often causes it would have
disappeared. If the second plan were adopted, it
would not cost the firm inaugurating it much more
than the slight expenses for clerical work involved in
keeping the accounts for the system. It would re-
move another objection sometimes considered a bar
to the hiring of older women—to wit, the fear that
they may need to be pensioned before they have rendered sufficiently long service to the concern that
engages them. Since they are paying the greater part
of their own annuities these cannot then justly be
considered a burden to the firm. It would give workers who, for any reason, leave a concern before retiring age a fund on which to start anew, which they
themselves have saved. It would at the same time
operate against any tendency to excessive turnover,
since workers would not be so apt to withdraw from
a concern through which their funds were invested.
And it would not need to cost the State very much,
for the administration of such a system could be
made part of the work of the State Insurance Department.

This proposed plan has some of the general features of an unemployment insurance system, inas-

much as weekly premiums would be deducted from the employees' pay to cover their annuity cost, with perhaps some contribution from employers. The aggregate of any given employee's deductions to the date of her separation from work could be used to tide her over periods of worklessness, as would any unemployment insurance fund. It differs from most unemployment insurance programmes insofar as it does not require the firm to cover the expenses of the workers' periods of idleness, and inasmuch as it requires neither State contributions to an annuity fund nor contributions to such a fund, necessarily, from employers. It is in its essence really a system of compulsory saving, to which the employees can hardly object since they themselves would at all times be the beneficiaries. State supervision would insure the safe investment and disbursement of the accruals. A method could even be devised whereby workers could borrow against their accumulated sum in times of special need as they now do on a life insurance policy.

A pension system like the one outlined would not be difficult to inaugurate. It would probably be opposed neither by the employers nor by the workers, since it inflicts no great expense on the former—especially if employers' contributions be omitted entirely; and it does not have the taint of paternalism that makes some State insurance schemes obnoxious to the latter. Some form of State pension system is a crying need in industry, that older salaried workers may have the comparative economic security that years of service with a concern merit, and which many firms would be only too willing to adopt were the State to take the initiative.

VII

One of the oldest department stores in the city recently underwent reorganization, owing to the death of its founder. During his lifetime a pension fund had been established which seemed to be built on a solid foundation, and which therefore promised employees long with the firm immunity from want once they became too old to serve. Old employees used to receive bonuses at Christmas time, beginning with a modest sum after ten years of service and going upward proportionately as the years of service increased. Workers who had been long with the firm were recognized as having had a part in its growth; and the recognition of their contribution to the firm's progress was regarded as a matter of course.

The will of the founder made certain bequests to old employees. It also made certain stipulations regarding the continuance of policies to protect these workers. But in spite of all these safeguards the position of the older employees in this concern is growing steadily more untenable.

Why is this so? Apparently there has come about under the new management a change of attitude regarding older workers. The recent experience of one of their older saleswomen may be cited as an example. Some slight disagreement with the floor manager over the delaying of a lunch hour until four o'clock was allowed to develop into resignation from the firm—this after more than twenty years of faithful service. She was permitted to go without a word of regret or appreciation, without any attempt to adjust the difficulty that caused her departure. Her pension rights were forfeited with her withdrawal.

One serious element in the employment policies of this shop as far as the workers in it are concerned was tersely indicated by its employment manager when she pointed out that the workers well understood that theirs was a day to day contract only. How any *esprit de corps* could possibly be found or expected in an organization where that is the case, it is difficult to comprehend. It is particularly hard for older employees in this concern to adjust themselves to such conditions since those to which they were previously accustomed were so very different.

Two remedies for situations of this kind suggest themselves, both of which could be inaugurated and enforced by the State. First, disputes involving the possible discharge of workers, in cases where employees were not unionized, could be brought before a State Board of Review, and there considered before the discharge became effective. Secondly, it could be made obligatory on all firms to give employees they intended to discharge at least two weeks' notice.

The unfortunately impersonal organization of

most concerns at the present time makes it easy to forget that, though an employee's time may be paid for at the market rate, the good will and the effort that spring from a personal pride and interest in the firm's welfare, and that reflect themselves in devoted service, are frequently not included in estimating wage rates. It is this element of personal devotion that wins for the employee the right to be considered as an individual in the event of difficulties that may cost him his means of livelihood. He has not been fully paid for his services if only his weekly wage is given him, without the accompaniment of any appreciation of his value as a personal factor in the concern's operation. Nor can even an impersonal corporation reach its greatest heights of success unless it somehow wins the confidence of its workers that it regards them as people and not merely as machines.

While the State is hardly the agency to which to look either for the inculcation of this feeling or a demonstration of the need for it, the State can enact legislation to protect employees against the insecurity of day to day tenure in commercial establishments. It needs no argument to demonstrate the unfairness to employees that is the result of asking them to work with a perpetual sword of Damocles hanging over their heads. Nor does the concern itself fail to lose where such a system is in force. Legislation like that suggested would give the employees opportunity to adjust the difficulty that threatens their position; or, failing that, to look about for another post. It would make upper clerks and under officials generally who sometimes make work very unpleasant for their subordinates, more careful about the dismissal notices they issue, since such action would need to be justified before an impartial board. And the concerns themselves could hardly fail to gain from legislation that steadies the morale of its labor force.

VIII

There are no doubt some older women who possess the necessary qualifications and experience to succeed as shop-keepers, but who through no fault of their own lack the necessary capital. Is there no way in which these women could be started on the road to success?

Would it not be possible to establish, either through State aid or as a private enterprise, a fund on which older women who could give the necessary references could draw for this purpose? Could not a mortgage on the business, with an amortization clause operating over a term of years, be made security for such a loan?

There are at present privately run loan associations that try to do something of this kind. But they frequently charge a considerable part of the loan as a bonus in the first place, and then arrange for repayment of the full face value of the loan on such terms as to make it entirely collectable within a year. The fund suggested could be operated so as to eliminate the bonus, and to make loans for a term of years at as low an interest rate as market conditions allowed. The amortization feature would gradually but surely decrease the risk by reducing the amount of the loan with each payment. As for the older woman concerned, it would gradually make it possible for her to own the business free and clear.

A precedent for government aid of this type already exists. The Federal Farm Loan banks have as their object the making of loans to farmers who wish to buy improved machinery or other farm supplies. The number of such banks, the details of their organization and administration, and the general terms for making loans, are determined by the Federal Farm Loan Board. This Board consists of the Secretary of the Treasury and six other members, chosen by the President with the advice and consent of the Senate. But the banks themselves are private enterprises, selling bonds to the public as does any other corporation. These banks charge one per cent more for making loans than they pay to their bondholders. It is calculated that this one per cent, put to work through a fund designated for this purpose, earns a sum equal to the whole amount of the loan in forty years. Thus the burden on the taxpayers for this work is comparatively light.

There are some essential points of difference be-

tween the security back of a farm loan and that
suggested for the proposed loans to women retail
shop-keepers. These would undoubtedly affect somewhat the organization of a fund from which to
finance such loans. The farmer's business, for instance, is already established. His land is security
for any loan he takes. In the case of the proposed
loans to older women, the very establishment of
the enterprise would be contingent on the obtaining
of a loan. The security offered to cover the loan
would be a mortgage on the stock purchased with
its proceeds. That is, in the last analysis, actually
lending the stock outright. But is this procedure as
risky as it sounds?

Let us assume that a succession of poor crops
makes it impossible for the farmer to meet his
interest payments. Foreclosure will result. The
amount realized from the consequent forced sale of
his farm will probably cover the amount of the
mortgage on it; for in most cases the amount loaned
was kept at a sufficiently balanced ratio to its as-
sessed value to make this fairly certain. Thus these
loans to farmers are comparatively safe. In the case
of the proposed loans to be made to older women
for the operation of retail shops, failure to meet
the interest terms would, too, result in foreclosure.
The stocks in these shops would probably be either
seasonable or perishable. Therefore the amount
realized by a forced sale would in many cases fall
short of the sum loaned. But it will be recalled

that these loans, before they were made, were endorsed or underwritten by a commercially responsible person. Therefore the fund would get back the amount of its loan in full. Any resultant loss would be borne by the underwriter.

The element of risk is, then, not much greater in the case of these loans than is the situation with the farm loans. If sufficient care is exercised in the placing of the loans, losses need be neither frequent nor large. Privately run loan associations, which frankly want to make as much money as possible out of the service they render, have no hesitation in making loans of this type. But, as has before been indicated, even though these associations are willing to make them, the short time during which they usually run and the high interest rate and bonus features make them of doubtful service to the older woman. An organization run under the direct supervision of the State and desiring to win only a moderate amount of profit might safely undertake the enterprise, and at the same time be of great service.

It may be urged that, since there are comparatively few older women who would require the aid of such a fund, it would therefore not be worth the effort to organize. In the case of the farmers, these are numerous; and their services are important for every person in the land, city dweller or otherwise. So whatever benefits them directly benefits every one else. But the older women are only a small group.

Carrying such a fund for them would be caring especially for a disproportionate section of the people.

Of course, such a fund could be worked out as part of a much wider State loan scheme. But as to its lack of importance because of the relatively small number of people affected, it might just as logically be argued that because most of the members of a community are prosperous, the expense of caring for the comparatively few members who are not is unwarranted. Farmers are far more numerous than older women wishing to open retail shops who lack the necessary capital. But not every farmer avails himself of the privileges extended by the farm loan banks. Nor is the bankruptcy of any particular farmer any more important to the public at large than is the failure of any one older woman to get on her feet. Yet, as it is impossible for the human body to function perfectly even if one tooth be painful, so is the social body handicapped if even a small group of its members functions less fully from the economic standpoint than it might. Even if the proposed loan fund were to be established without the underwriting feature, must it then be abandoned? Is not the slight risk involved well worth the taking, if the successful outcome of such a scheme promises some of its citizens economic stability? Is not such a loss, even were it certain to be incurred, cheaper in the long run than the possible later entire care of some of these older women?

IX

Of the aids to older workers, and especially to the older woman, here outlined, none are especially difficult or very expensive to put into effect. Such a programme of State legislation could, without offense on the score of paternalism, eradicate many of the unfavorable elements that now complicate the problem of the older woman's position in industry.

Nor would the State need to be very militant in carrying out such legislation. The very existence of regulations to counteract some of the tendencies that now hamper older people, including women, would safeguard their positions where that was necessary. And would not the fact that its older citizens retained their economic effectiveness be a more than adequate recompense to the State for any effort or expenditure that might be needed to secure this end?

CHAPTER IV

THE PROBLEM IN ITS SOCIAL ASPECTS

I

"For years the theory has stubbornly persisted," says the Director of the Women's Bureau of the United States Department of Labor, "that women are in industry for only a short time, and that their earnings are of no very great social significance because 'the family,' the unit of modern civilization, is dependent upon woman not as a wage earner but as a home-keeper. More and more, however, modern industrial studies show that women wage earners have a double social significance. It is found that they are contributing a by no means insignificant proportion of the family wage, in many cases being the entire support of a good-sized family, while at the same time they are fulfilling their age-old function of home-keeper."*

This bureau finds that in the country as a whole three-fifths of the number of working women in it are more than twenty-five years old; that one-third of the domestic workers are forty-five years old or more, and that one-fifth of all the married women

* "Short Talks About Working Women." Washington, D. C., March, 1927, p. 11.

who are employed are forty-five years old or over.*
We have found that approximately one-third of all
the women employed in Greater New York were
thirty-five years old or over. The social importance
of employment tenure for this army of workers is
apparent. When it is considered that older women
frequently have others besides themselves to support, the far-reaching effects of a lack of employment tenure for them can hardly be questioned.

Those older women who are denied entrance or
reinstatement in industry may not yet form a very
great segment of the total number of middle-aged
workers. But from present indications there is little
reason to expect that the tendency shown by some
concerns to bar all older women from employment
through arbitrary age limit barriers will suddenly
be abandoned. On the contrary, it is not at all certain that it will not spread to more and more firms
with the coming years, unless business men in the
meantime come to realize that the pursuance of
such a policy will redound to their own financial
detriment.

It has already been pointed out that firms who
bar inefficient older women are pursuing a perfectly
understandable policy. It can hardly be expected
that any firm will deliberately clog the machinery
of its own organization by the retention of workers incompetent to render satisfactory service to it.

* Report of the Director of the Women's Bureau, U. S. Dept. of
Labor, Washington, D. C., 1925, p. 10.

The social injury is not here, but in the automatic barring out of all older workers who have reached years in many cases still short of middle age, as that term is generally accepted. The social loss comes through the stultification of workers who still have many years of effective effort to give to industry.

The financial loss to firms who follow age discrimination policies is often felt directly through their high turnover costs and through the lowered level of sales and contacts that result from the entrusting of intricate commercial transactions to less experienced subordinates than might have been hired. But there is also an indirect financial loss— that incurred because business is not as "good" in some fields as it might be.

This is the natural and inevitable effect of worklessness among any considerable group of wage-earners. Older women who have no positions must cut down their budgets for food, clothing, and other personal expenses in the retail establishments they patronize. These shops reflect their lessened business in the form of reduced orders to the wholesale firms that supply them. The wholesale firms in turn buy less raw materials, curtail their manufactured output, and consequently lay off some of their workers. Somewhere along the line the losses must reach also those concerns that discriminate against older women.

Nor is this all. Illness is much more likely to step

in where weakness, induced by worry and lack of proper nourishment, exist than in cases where the worker is free from mental strain and is physically strong. When it strikes the home of a workless older woman, she must, however reluctantly, apply to the public medical authorities for aid. The needs of these institutions are met by taxing, among others, those who operate business concerns in the community. Obviously, the more expenses these institutions have, the higher the taxes these employers will need to pay. For instance, an article appearing in the New York *Times* of February 5, 1928, quotes the Comptroller of the State of New York as estimating that the cost of maintaining the State welfare organizations will double in the next thirty years if the present rate of increase of dependents is maintained. That cost now amounts to about $250,000,000 a year for the care of 64,114 persons. With many older women unable to find means of support for themselves and their dependents, are we not unduly hopeful when we trust that the present rate of increase will merely be maintained? Must we not rather face its undoubted growth? And those firms practising discrimination must share, along with the others, the increased levies necessitated by this growth.

The net social result of a policy that tends to work injury to any one group is lowered efficiency throughout the whole body of which it is a part. But the lessened financial returns that are inevitable through such a policy, and the lessened material welfare of the whole fabric affected by the workless members, are not the worst social losses that follow. Much more serious is the break in morale that comes not from the lowering of the workers' financial standing, but from the realization that business has cast them off as no longer of service to it.

Any policy that brings the shadow of such a realization to the heart of any human being is the essence of cruelty. Laws are formulated to protect private property. Public indignation follows the wresting of it from any member of the community. Powerful machinery is put in motion to catch the offender. Public money for his maintenance is spent for years that he may not be free to practise his depredations on additional members. Physical violence is equally condemned, and the offender is prevented at the public expense from perpetrating more such acts. Yet policies that injure far more deeply—that break the faith of workers in themselves and their value—are allowed to be carried out unchecked. They are, in effect, performing spiritual murder. *Mut verloren, Alles verloren,* says the German proverb; it presents the results of such a policy exactly.

Business concerns that have helped to bring about the establishment of industrial age limits no doubt feel, where they consider the matter at all, that the workers they bar can readily find work elsewhere.

That might perhaps be true were they the only ones to refuse to hire them. But where such procedure is beginning to spread generally and is already definitely established in one large industry, namely, clerical work, it has the effect on workers still comparatively young of turning toward them a concerted and united front which they must despair of ever penetrating.

Some unusually able people, confronted with shut doors on looking for employment after the thirty-five year mark has been passed, may no doubt be stung by the situation into activity which will ultimately lead them further than the acquisition of a position might have done. At the other end of the middle-aged scale are workers poor in health, in training, in determination, or in personality, and perhaps unable therefore to render much valuable service to any concern—the more or less unemployable who must be cared for in other ways. Both of these are relatively small groups. But the great bulk of older workers are those of average ability. They are the steady, dependable people who are by nature and temperament fitted for routine positions. Some have more initiative and greater executive ability than others, so that within this group are women who can fill comparatively responsible positions as well as those who are better adapted for the simpler kinds of work. But each in her place is a potential commercial asset for some concern—far too valuable to cast upon the scrap heap.

Industry has evolved methods of turning what was formerly waste in manufacturing, into by-products that sometimes exceed in commercial returns those from the main material it puts out. The gains from commercial endeavor have been poured into research laboratories for the lessening of human physical suffering. Hours have been shortened, better equipped plants built, recreational facilities for workers provided, because it is now generally known that these things in the long run bring better financial returns for the concerns that employ them. Yet in the midst of all these constructive elements, the operation of which helps both industry and the employees engaged in it, there is growing up this destructive idea that women over thirty or thirty-five years old have no more useful work in their specialties to offer to industry.   On humanitarian grounds the wholesale blocking out of older women from employment is indefensible; on economic grounds it is bad commercial practice. On what grounds can it be justified? On those who practise it rests the burden of its defense.

Is this a problem for society to consider? Is it not rather the concern of industry alone? But has not the *laissez-faire* idea long ago been disproved in connection with the relations between employer and employee? Is not the mass of protective legislation that has grown up around the worker in the past century ample proof that *laissez-faire* in dealing with employees is no longer regarded as tenable by enlightened governments? Does not the contribution by the worker of the best that is in him put upon the employer who obtains this service, and upon the community as a whole, the moral obligation to respect on their part the worker's right to function as an industrial factor?

Women of thirty or thirty-five have all contributed years of effort to industry before reaching that age. If they have been engaged in home duties they have given service that, compensated on the basis of similar work done by a hired employee, would have been translated into terms of definite financial value. Those who have had positions outside of the home have had tangible financial returns to show for their effort. Both have by their work given impetus to the material and the social progress of the community of which they are a part—a community that has been built up because every one in it has so contributed. Can the community in effect now turn about and without further obligation to them cast them off? Must it not study the plight in which this group now finds itself, not patronizingly, not in the spirit of "uplift," but seriously as it would study illness on the part of a member whose economic and social value it recognizes and wishes to retain?

II

At a banquet recently held for its older employees by a great electrical concern, James J. Davis,

United States Secretary of Labor, was the speaker. Naturally enough, on such an occasion his talk centered on the value of older employees to business. After giving as reasons for the additional value of older workers to their concerns their greater experience and skill, and dwelling on the changed attitude toward the capacities of older people that had been brought about by more scientific methods of living, he went on to say:

"In the face of this tendency of science and our better life to abolish age and keep us young and even more productive, we have a tendency among employers to drop good workers at an ever younger and younger age. I think it is something that is serious and should be watched."*

Undoubtedly it is just that—serious from the social as well as from the economic standpoint. There are few people so callous as to be unable to feel the injustice and the cruelty that lie in labelling workers as "too old" to function in industry just when they have developed to the point of contributing of their best. It is hard to understand how gifted business men could have been blind enough to their own gains in production to pursue such a policy, unless it can be explained on the aforementioned ground of the impersonal organization of large scale groups to whom individual workers and their contribution to industry signify nothing. That the workers mean nothing to them is not so because

* New York *Times*, January 29, 1928.

the people at the head of these organizations are individually monsters of greed. Rather do they mean nothing because modern business organization has become a fever of merging, consolidating, and absorbing, that has left in most corporations a feeling of restlessness, a tendency to regard their present status as merely temporary. Under such circumstances personnel can mean but little, low payroll figures much. The aim of old-time business men to build up industries that later would bear their name and stand as a monument to their business acumen, has become a nightmare of greater and greater expansion and absorption, in which the name of any individual means little, while the power and the added wealth to be acquired through the mass application of gigantic aggregations of capital, mean everything.

The full effect socially of the rearing of these top-heavy commercial superstructures can not yet be evaluated. One result, however, stands before us now. Its lengthening shadow threatens to spread over what is commonly regarded as the "backbone" of any nation—its group of serious, experienced, skilled workers, both men and women. Are not organizations which with one hand build up superstructures of commerce and with the other throttle the buying power of what must be a large section of its consuming public, themselves creating the weak spot that, given time to corrode, may be a fruitful cause of their future crumbling? The social hurt through such failures must needs be tremendous. Through the sale of their stock these large-scale corporations have spread their roots through the length and breadth of the economic life of the country. Therefore they cannot suffer injury without at the same time transmitting pain throughout the entire economic system.

Stretching luxuriously in their giant strength, they may hardly know at the moment that the motion of their mighty arms is crushing to the earth the older men and women of industry. Perhaps to them these older people may seem of no consequence. But that is an untenable point. If vision and genius are the forces back of the construction of large-scale business enterprises—and few will deny that they enter into it—just as surely the realization of these visions must be in large measure in the hands of the workers whose concerted efforts and co-operation must be won before these dreams can find fulfillment. Nor can the quality of a product rise above this contribution of the individual worker who, no matter how wisely he is directed, how carefully watched, how mechanicalized into human machine power, still remains an important element in production. Does not the shutting out of its abler, more expert and more mature workers inevitably lower the level of the products offered to society?

III

Foundations have been created that have for their purpose the salvaging of human material. With this end in view they have extended their studies to the bettering of health and housing conditions, and to improving working conditions generally for employees, in order that these may marshal at their best all their latent abilities for the service of industry. It has long since been established that lessened labor misunderstandings and the greater satisfaction of the worker with the conditions of his employment have resulted in gains that have more than balanced the unavoidable expenses incurred in tackling industrial problems scientifically. A comparatively new problem has now presented itself—namely, the value of the middle-aged woman to industry. It needs careful study and research. The many angles it presents must be studied separately. It must be authoritatively established how the older woman's net output compares with that of younger workers of the same general background, education, and technical training. It must be demonstrated by wide-spread inquiry how great is the loss from turnover among young workers as compared with the saving that results from the retaining of steady workers who are older. It must be shown how extensively her economic welfare affects those who are dependent on her efforts. It must be pointed out how the welfare of all this group is tied up economically and socially with the welfare of society at large.

Careful study, too, must be made of the ways in which older workers may best be classified as to their skill, and how this may be ramified and improved and strengthened. A campaign of education through newspaper and magazine articles and through lecture courses is urgently needed quite as much to acquaint the older woman with her relation to business as to bring before the public at large the nature of her problem. The following letter, reprinted from the New York *Sun* of January 27, 1928, shows this need vividly enough:

PAST 30 AND FULL OF PEP

Another Inquirer About the Problem of Landing the Job.

To the What Do You Think Editor:

Sir: Are there many women like myself who in the late thirties are full of pep and go and yet have had no training to earn their own living?

I have tried registry offices, but they are worse than useless; indeed some of them are sufficient to develop inferiority complexes in older women even if they hadn't them before. To have an efficient young girl fix a relentless eye on you and then give you a cool stare when you have to admit that you have not had training or experience outside your own home!

Two clergymen told me that I should have no difficulty in getting a job because "you can't buy dependableness and trustworthiness" one of them said. The other remarked, "an efficient woman such as you will have no difficulty." There it ended.

Self-praise is no recommendation, but here goes! I am methodical, quick and adaptable. I have done any amount of secretarial and clerical work in my own home. I have looked after maids and done the work when they were absent or non-existent. I have traveled and met people of many nationalities.

I want to keep my own little home, but isn't there some other way I can earn my living than stand in a store all day or engage in that most deadly of· all jobs offered to the older woman—selling things on commission?

CHEERFUL, THOUGH PUZZLED.

Letters like this are among the things that make it hard for older women to prove their value to the satisfaction of business men. Just what this woman, or the clergymen who advised her, expect industry to do in her case it would be interesting to discover. Apparently she could find work in selling; but either she was blind to its possibilities or else she had no liking or aptitude for it. Yet her letter indicates that, if she were properly enlightened as to the right of industry to demand preparation from those who desire a place in it, and carefully directed as to the best way to make use of her special experiences, she might in time prove valuable to it.

Foundation and research bureaus that undertook the work of studying the older woman's position in industry as an industrial problem would find that it falls automatically into two parts—(1) those elements that affect the inexperienced woman, and (2) those that concern the woman who has had some years of business training. In both groups certain general lines, such as the development of desirable traits in personality and a knowledge of certain general principles of business procedure and requirements, would coincide. But beyond these, the methods of making each group best realize its own possibilities would of necessity differ widely.

In such study the aid of already existing machinery, such as the Women's Bureau of the United States Department of Labor and the Bureau of Women in Industry of the New York State Department of Labor, would prove invaluable. Requests for comprehensive statistical material in connection with older women in the employ of various concerns would, if made by them, yield full replies and therefore much information. Existing facilities for Government printing and franking would insure the wide distribution of material gathered and tabulated by these bureaus. The desires of the Government would be sufficient to gain wide-spread newspaper publicity for any angle of the situation that it felt was particularly desirable to have brought before the public. The bending of the forces of the already existing Government agencies and private foundations to a study of this problem would aid in its solution as few other means would have the power to do.

IV

At present* the country is faced with a serious unemployment problem. The worklessness of the group of older women shut out by age limits forms a considerable factor in it. But their idleness has in it an element of grimness fortunately absent from the situation in general. For while the bulk of unemployment will disappear once business conditions again right themselves, the worklessness of older women threatens to remain permanent as a result of the fact that their unemployment is based on a set policy.

It must have occurred to many who are interested in the older woman's industrial fate to wonder what can possibly become of her should age limit discriminations bar her for any length of time and in great numbers. Let it be assumed that the barriers erected against women over thirty-five years old be raised before the doors of employment offices in greater and ever increasing strength. There are more than 100,000 of these women in Manhattan Borough, and almost 200,000 in Greater New York, engaged in five occupations alone—the selling, clerical, domestic, manufacturing and transportation fields. That is a large enough group to make self-evident the importance socially of any policy that affects their economic welfare. What would be the

* Spring, 1928.

effect on society in general, let us say in Greater New York, were this large segment of its workers to meet with increasing difficulty in finding or retaining employment?

The median full time earnings of women in New York City in two industries—the factory and the mercantile fields—are given by the New York State Women's Bureau* as $18.25 for each. The distribution of the earnings in the mercantile field, adapted from this source, is shown in Figure XVI.

If we accept the median of $18.25 as the average wage of the woman over thirty-five years old in New York City, the maximum loss to this class of workers, assuming wide-spread unemployment. for them, would total approximately $3,650,000 per week, or $189,800,000 for the full time period of fifty-two weeks. That is in general the amount of spending power that would be lost to these women for their living expenses. But the bulk of these expenses go on during the life-time of the older woman. If she has no relatives to give her shelter, no source of income outside of her earnings, and—as is quite likely in view of her low average wage—no sum set aside to tide her over years of idleness, this yearly sum of approximately $189,800,000 for New York City alone must somehow be covered by the community. What the extent of it would be for the entire country, were we to estimate the wide-spread

* "Hours and Earnings of Women in Five Industries." State of New York Dept. of Labor, Bureau of Women in Industry, Nov., 1923.

operation of a policy of exclusion for older women to its full extent, can easily be conceived from this example. But to consider New York City alone is enough to bring to the minds of business men as well as to the general public the extent of the loss of business that must be shouldered by the community because a group of its members, due to exclusion measures, cannot properly care for themselves.

The sum quoted, large as it is, does not, however, cover all the phases of the situation. For presum-

FIGURE XVI

EARNINGS OF FULL TIME WORKERS, MERCANTILE,
NEW YORK CITY

Adapted from New York State Dept. of Labor, Bulletin No. 131, 1923

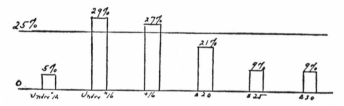

ably, whatever form public care may take for a time, eventually some of these women must reach the stage where public institutions must shelter them. Assuming that only one-half of this number will require this aid, then, on the basis of the estimated cost of $900 a year* for caring for each aged

* *American Labor Legislation Review*, Dec., 1927. "Old Age Pension Legislation."

person in a home, the expense to the State for one year for 100,000 persons in New York City alone would be $90,000,000—a not inconsiderable budget for the State to pay in one field for one city.

These figures take the problem at what is probably close to its maximum. At no time is it likely that all women of thirty-five or older will simultaneously be barred from employment. But from present indications, unless industry takes cognizance of the varied types of costs to itself that must result from a continuance and an extension of the policy of denying the older woman work, there must inevitably fall upon it some share of the large amount that would be involved in caring for any section of so numerous a group of workers.

If they cannot work, and if they have no one to support them, what else but to become public charges is left for women who at thirty-five years of age can no longer find places in industrial plants? Not the limited number of women who for personal or physical reasons may be unemployable, and who must therefore be otherwise cared for—not the equally limited number of able women whose abilities are greater than the strength of the forces directed against them and who can therefore find ways to surmount them—but the bulk of average, every-day women, good, strong, self-respecting workers who form the rank and file of female labor, these are the ones who at thirty-five years old are faced with the blind wall of idleness which, unless they escape by some niche not at present observable, is not unlikely to extend over a period of thirty-five or forty years.

It seems almost incredible that such a condition, even in any degree, could be tolerated. The situation is, as Pope observed long ago in another connection,

> " . . . a monster of so frightful mien,
> As, to be hated, needs but to be seen."

Would not reflection on the part of industries as to their own direct and indirect losses in pursuing the policy of erecting these arbitrary age limits, help meet it? These women do not want to be a tax on the society of which they form a part. On the contrary, they want to contribute with the rest to its maintenance. Full of the desire to work, in the strength of their maturity, they ask that this thing that has come upon them be studied, be analyzed, and, if their cause be found just, be moved from the path of their industrial welfare. As members of society they ask that it consider their case. All society, as well as the older women directly concerned, must pay the bill for the loss of their services to industry. All society gains if they contribute them. Society can only profit if it succeeds in unraveling this tangle that threatens to ensnare beyond escape so large a group of its members.

CHAPTER V

THE SOLUTIONS SOME OLDER WOMEN FOUND

I

In the foregoing considerations of the middle-aged woman in industry we have pointed out some of the difficulties she encounters in her search for a foothold; and we have endeavored to indicate some of the reasons for these difficulties. But some older women have risen triumphantly over all obstacles to a place of economic safety for themselves and their dependents. How did they do it?

First in the field of industrial successes scored by the older woman is the conducting of retail shops. The Fourteenth Federal Census gives the number of retail shops in Manhattan alone owned by women of twenty-five or over as 2,594. Of these 1,552 belong to women between the ages of twenty-five and forty-four; 927 to those between forty-five and sixty-four, and 115 to women of sixty-five and over. Taking one-half of the twenty-five to forty-four year group and adding it to the rest, we find that approximately 1,818 women thirty-five years old or more operate retail shops in Manhattan.

These are of considerable variety. To enumerate them is also to indicate the increase in occupations for women that the last twenty-five years have brought about. To the millinery, bakery, confectionery and small dry goods shops of other days have been added beauty shops; gift, dress, curio, and novelty jewelry shops; antique shops; laundries; specialty shops for women's gloves and hosiery, and others for blouses and silk underwear; book and stationery shops; tea rooms of all kinds; interior decorating shops; florists' shops; travel bureaus; real estate and insurance agencies; and bond selling houses. To this list must be added business schools, and institutions that teach manicuring, hair dressing, lampshade making, crochet beading, and hotel service work.

Most of the older women operating these shops were once employees in similar organizations. But middle age, instead of seeing them continuing as workers hired by others, found them firmly established in their own right.

It took courage for these women to accomplish this. It took thrift and self-denial to accumulate the capital on which they could start. It required tenacity of purpose to help them over the hard beginning months. It needed good taste for a wise choice of stock. It required, above all, a pleasant personality to win and to hold their customers.

Some of the small shops expanded in the course of time into larger establishments; others remained small. The extent of their success varied with the amount of capital they were able to invest, the number of rival establishments of similar type in the neighborhood, and the good taste and the general personality of the older woman in charge. But once established, the spectre of worklessness for these women was laid forever. They had made themselves independent—free of both age barriers and employment agencies.

To be sure, often there was worry connected with the operation of these shops. Sometimes there was not enough capital for expansion at a favorable moment. Occasionally a bad choice of stock led to consequent losses. Sometimes a bad business year was hard to survive. Sometimes unseasonable weather so retarded sales that even well-chosen stocks had to be disposed of at considerable price reductions. But these difficulties, incident to all business concerns, were no worse for the older woman than for any one else; and they could usually be surmounted by judgment, persistence, and patience—qualities in which many an older woman was particularly well schooled.

Moreover, these difficulties, while causing the older woman undoubted anxiety, were very different in type from the cares that beset her when, losing one position, she could not tell whether she would ever obtain another. Nor did these struggles injure her self-confidence and break her self-respect as did the discouraging hunt for work that so many middle-aged women had learned to dread. On the contrary, they tended to develop her personality. For the independent shop-keeper, in order to maintain herself, was forced to make her own decisions, to use her own initiative. She was compelled to undergo the hard work of doing her own planning instead of merely obeying the orders that represented some one else's thinking. The net effect of her attempts to overcome the drawbacks that beset her was stimulating and strengthening rather than exhausting.

It is quite true that the older women who succeed in independent store-keeping do so, not because they are middle aged, but because they .are capable. Yet many more women who now go their discouraged round from office to shop could succeed in this work were they to make the effort. If they know well any special type of goods or services and have some initial capital, the returns through applying them in this way would, in all probability, be at least as great as the salary they might earn in another's employ. Besides, they have the added and inestimable joy of being the arbiters of their own commercial fate rather than the passive factors in another's decision.

II

Older women operating retail establishments often follow the present trend in this field toward

chain store organization. The most obvious types of
shops for such development are hat shops, dress
shops, beauty shops, and tea rooms and other establishments primarily interested in the production of
foodstuffs.

One distinguished success was scored by an older
woman, who, left a widow in her forties with very
small means, conceived the idea of opening a coffee shop. Not only was the coffee she served so
delicious that it soon became widely known, but the
surroundings and the service, too, were unusual.
Since she had the wisdom to establish herself in the
heart of the theatre district, she had a potential
trade in that fact alone. Also, the large retail mercantile establishments and the crowded office-build-
ings in this locality assured her of a continuous flow
of patronage to which the matinée groups need be
no more than an addition.

Besides the delicious refreshments for which her
shop soon became noted, she operated in it a small,
moderately priced but tasteful gift shop. This last
was inaugurated for the convenience of the many
theatre-goers who lived outside the city, and who
desired to take home some slight remembrance for
friends. It helped decidedly to make the whole venture a success.

Originally a small shop, this coffee room has
grown into five good-sized restaurants. But the woman operating them is not yet content. She now
markets in addition, on a fairly large scale, the par-

ticular blend of coffee that was the foundation of her first shop's success.

Another venture, smaller in scope but no less illustrative, is a cake-shop operated by several sisters. They began modestly in a small store on upper Broadway. Here lived many young matrons who gave frequent card parties and afternoon teas for which fine cakes were often required. Since many of the apartments occupied by these young women were cared for by maids to whom baking was an unknown art, and since their mistresses were disinclined to do this work themselves, the sisters who opened this shop had an almost immediate success. This was all the easier for them because their products were really good. It was not long before a second shop was opened not far from the first; and now there are four, all flourishing.

The interesting thing about this particular venture was the fact that it required very little initial capital. It was the business acumen and the general intelligence of these older women that, added to their culinary talents, gave them independence and at the same time a reputation for some of the best products of their kind.

A third success is the one made by another group of sisters, this time in the "beauty culture" field. Beginning in the days before bobbed hair became the vogue, they were, with the aid of judicious advertising and the invention of some hair tonics, already well started when hair bobbing and trimming established them still more firmly. These sisters now operate several branches. Their success is duplicated by many others in the same field.

There is one example of a chain shop which is interesting because of the possibilities it suggests for middle-aged women. It is a retail candy chain. The corporation that operates it may have had its inception in a tiny kitchen run by an older woman. But whether or not this was so, this corporation realized that at any rate it should have been. So it chose as its trade name a simple one that somehow suggested a capable older woman. Reluctant to rely on the effect of this alone, it printed on the covers of its containers the picture of a dear, motherly soul whose aspect reminded one at once of the smell of fresh chocolate and simmering molasses. Nor did the ingenuity of this corporation stop here. It devised a uniform dress for all its shops in order further to carry out the idea of homely simplicity. The interior and the woodwork of the exterior are painted white; all the shelves are white; and the windows are curtained in white muslin studded with black dots. One more master stroke was added to this ensemble. That was the featuring of the type of candies usually known as "old-fashioned."

As may readily be perceived by the older woman, this example shows that, so far from being a commercial detriment, middle age may sometimes be a distinct asset. Therefore she need not despair.

Schools for imparting some form of commercial

technic often give the older woman an excellent opportunity to establish herself independently. In this field, too, her age is more an asset than a liability, because a middle-aged woman inspires confidence in her experience and ability to do this kind of work.

Some of these schools are organized for instruction in office technic, such as filing, general secretarial work, and bookkeeping. The older women in charge of them have, as a rule, had years of business experience; but they did not wait for age barriers to be erected against them in clerical work.

Other women run schools for teaching hotel service work. These advertise extensively, and, where they are effectively operated, they can undoubtedly help older women, especially those without previous training, to qualify for good positions. They could also do much to help place them after they are trained. The older women in charge of these have also solved the employment problem as far as they themselves are concerned.

Some older women conduct schools for training experts in cooking and baking. The women who master this work are expected to fill positions in hotels, restaurants and tea rooms, as dieticians in hospitals or other institutions, or as upper cooks in large homes. The women at the head of such institutions have, as a rule, already won a reputation in the work they impart. Usually this has been gained through the publication of cook books, or through the extensive advertising of special recipes.

A few older women care in their homes for the small children of working mothers. This field, however, is not yet much cultivated by older women, even though, unlike many others, this is not a new occupation for them. Probably they do not find it lucrative enough in proportion to the strain and effort necessarily employed in following it.

Older women who are expert in cutting and dressmaking sometimes teach these things to other women. That is true also of millinery, lampshade making, and crochet beading. Some trained in manicuring and hairdressing operate schools for preparing other women to take up this work.

These occupations all mark an advance for the older women engaged in them. These women are no longer in the ranks of their middle-aged sisters seeking work; they are, in many cases, in a position to give work to others. It is hoped that none of these, now that they are independent, erect age barriers.

Does clerical work offer no chance of independence to the older woman? If she is an expert stenographer and typist, and is besides intelligent and possessed of executive ability, she has a splendid field open to her as a public stenographer. In this work she sells her stenographic and typing services exactly as any other retail shop sells its stock in trade. If she is careful about the locality of her office and does good work, she will not be idle very frequently.

Most of the public stenographic offices are situated in or near the office-building centres, especially those housing law offices. Others prefer hotels. In the latter, the bulk of the work is usually done for the transient guests who, temporarily in the city on business, need the services of an expert stenographer during that time. Older women who maintain public stenographic offices frequently find them quite lucrative as a means of livelihood. Some are large enough to employ two or three assistants.

There are a few older women who maintain offices as visiting bookkeepers or accountants; but these are still comparatively rare. As a rule, the operation of secretarial schools and the conducting of public stenographic offices are the fields most frequently chosen by the older clerical worker who would be independent.

Many stenographers who do not wish to incur the responsibility of maintaining an office of their own have however, perfected themselves along one particular line. They are therefore in a position to offer expert service in it. Such workers are law stenographers, court stenographers, and foreign language stenographers. Though not entirely in a position of independence, they are comparatively well off in the competition for work, since they possess qualifications that fit them for employment with firms requiring more than routine office practice. Some clerical workers have passed civil service examinations, or found other appointments in some branch of government work, thus generally gaining life tenure and consequent freedom from employment cares.

An article in the New York *World* of November 27, 1927 describes another interesting field into which older women may advance from clerical positions. This is the work of the credit manager. There are already five hundred women on the membership roll of the national organization, although most of these are outside of New York City. However, two of the first women in the field were clerical workers in New York City shops before their advancement to this position. The article points out that this is a comparatively new field for women, for which their native tact, their love of detail work, their intuition, and their patience peculiarly fit them.

Other women who were formerly clerical workers have taken up personnel and placement work, and are to found following these vocations in department stores and particularly in employment agencies. But some older women, instead of taking positions with other agencies, have been courageous enough to open their own. In most cases these operate quite successfully, at any rate as far as their service in providing a source of livelihood for their owner is concerned.

Occasionally an older women who has had training in investment work opens an office of her own for trading in securities. Several women have built up very lucrative life insurance offices. Some women, too, have been very successful in conducting real estate agencies, particularly in the renting and the supervision of large apartment-houses and country estates.

The large number of older women who conduct successful dress, hat, and novelty jewelry shops is familiar to all consumers. Those who have learned not only how to sell these things but also something about the way they are made are in a much better position to profit by any sales opportunities that arise than are those who can point out to their customers only the surface features of their stocks. Good taste and an attractive personality are very important qualities here. The same characteristics much intensified are considerable factors in the success of the interior decorating establishments frequently found in the hands of middle-aged women.

The many dressmakers that work independently have already been mentioned. In Greater New York these number 12,409 women thirty-five years old or more. A number of them go out by the day, gradually building up a definite clientele whom they serve in this way at stated intervals. Some of them work alone in the small front room of the rather humble apartments they occupy in poor neighborhoods. Some rent small shops. Some maintain whole buildings or floors in exclusive neighborhoods given over to expensive specialty shops and requiring many assistants and subordinates. Whatever the size of the business they conduct, they work as independent factors, employing their ideas and their skill without supervision and without hindrance, able to retain their own profits, and governing their own hours of work within the limits of their customers' wishes. All of them, whatever medium they choose for their work, are far more advantageously placed than those who go the rounds of other women's shops or factories looking for positions, or bruising their self-respect against thirty-five year bars in employment agencies.

On the whole, it is all a very creditable showing, when one considers how brief woman's active commercial career has been. It is worthy of consideration by the older woman who is in despair about finding work, as well as by her sister who fears that she may at any time lose a position that she has perhaps held for years.

There is undoubtedly something that she can do very well—something, perhaps, that she would like to do rather than anything else. It may be very delicate handiwork. There are exchanges for women's work where she may dispose of this, if she does not wish to take the responsibility of operating her own shop. One such exchange, a modest little window in an old private house twenty-five years ago, is now quite an establishment, maintaining a large automobile delivery wagon for the sending out of its wares. There are, too, some older women engaged in the operation of this bureau.

Perhaps the older woman likes to put up preserves. Her grocer will probably allow her to keep a few jars on his counters in order to introduce them, if she arranges with him to retain a commission on all sales. If they are good preserves, and if she has chosen a grocer on whose co-operation she can depend and whose customers demand variety and excellent quality in the foodstuffs they buy, she will soon be kept busy supplying the demand.

Perhaps she is a former saleswoman who particularly likes shopping. She may find work with a shop or with a dressmaking house. But it is entirely possible for her to build up her own group of private customers, if she has a few good connections with which to start and does a little judicious advertising. There are a number of busy men and women, some of whom live at a considerable distance from large shopping centres, who would be glad to leave a part of their buying to an older woman on whose taste and judgment they could rely.

The middle-aged woman who is informed by agencies that there are no positions for her, or whom employment managers bar because they have decided that they want only young workers, need not necessarily feel that these pronouncements are her industrial death warrant. Such statements are merely opinions, reflecting what is probably only a passing economic phase. Why let them break her spirit? They are not immutable. Instead of allowing herself to be disheartened by them, let her regard them as a challenge to her abilities. Let her meet them. Let her take stock of her capabilities, and think of some way in which they may earn a livelihood for her. If she is determined to win, she will succeed in evolving something—even if it prove nothing more exciting in the beginning than operating a news-stand.

PART III

THE PROBLEM SUMMARIZED

CHAPTER I

ITS PRESENT PHASES—A RECAPITULATION

I

THE exigencies of modern economic and social life have forced into commercial activity thousands of older women who formerly would not have considered the likelihood of such a step. These modern trends have also kept in their positions many thousands of married older women who would formerly have devoted themselves to the care of the home or who would have assisted in the work of conducting some one else's.

All these women, some highly skilled in their various vocations, some quite inexperienced, find when they search for positions that a blank wall has been erected against them—the wall of arbitrary age limits. The tendency is to build this wall higher and higher not only against the older woman, but even against those who are still considered young women everywhere else but in employment offices. The maximum age of these barriers covers at present the range between twenty-five and thirty-five.

On the wrong side of the wall stretch years of potential labor power that just now is unable to scale the barrier. The wall operates to exclude not only the poorly qualified older woman but also the far greater number of able older women who must

231

find employment. At the same time it leaves wide open the gate of employment entrance to workers either still below the maximum age of the barrier or else willing to declare falsely that they are. The able ones among these young workers come in freely; but side by side with them come also the poorly equipped. Because of these conditions the following results to industry may be enumerated:

1. Industry, by excluding able workers through artificial age barriers, often robs itself of the opportunity to recruit the best possible employment force to carry on its work.

2. By choosing applicants on the basis of age, it hires many poorly equipped, slightly experienced, underdeveloped workers who, because they are inherently poor material and because they are badly trained or wholly untrained, do not apply themselves seriously. The result is loss from large labor turnover among young workers. The existence of this large turnover was practically everywhere admitted in those plants where personal visits were made.

3. This turnover is admitted generally to mean financial loss. Yet, on the statements of superintendents, practically no study has been made by them of this considerable financial leak.

4. Not only does loss from turnover result from the operation of this age limit policy, but the promiscuous types of workers chosen on the basis of mere age can hardly fail to turn out products in-

ferior to those that might have been made by workers chosen on the scores of personality and efficiency. The public consequently receives less return for its expenditures than would be the case were the goods made by the best available labor force.

II

When trying to find work older women may go from shop to shop and from factory to factory. They may register with agencies. They may insert or answer newspaper advertisements. Whichever medium they choose, the age barrier confronts them.

The growing tendency to erect these walls is not combated by the employment agencies to any appreciable degree, except in a few instances. That is because these agencies have in most cases hardly a conception of the great importance of the work they are attempting to do. They lack this consciousness because usually the training of the people operating them has not reached the level necessary for dealing with this matter of employment on a social plane. In most of them the angle of profit looms large, and the possibilities inherent in the work go unrecognized. Here and there sympathy for the older woman's plight is expressed by a placement manager. But it rarely occurs to any of them to take an active interest in solving a problem that may at any moment engulf them personally, for many of them are themselves middle-aged employees.

The State examination and license for those who wish to operate employment agencies or engage in personnel work in corporations, department stores or factories would, as heretofore suggested, tend to make them intelligent mediums for doing their work rather than mere purveyors of labor. Nor need the private agencies alone be thus improved. State employment bureaus, too, could be conducted by similarly licensed employees in a spirit of respect for the applicant and with the wish to help her, not as a "case," but as an equal.

The rare men or women who can work in this spirit and who possess the necessary training, may be expensive to obtain. But they would return to the State in value received far more than would be paid them in a salary budget. They are therefore well worth seeking out.

So far most of the emphasis on the State agencies, proposed or established, is placed on the relatively minor fact that they function without charge. But the work that lies in them to accomplish on the plane of actual personnel work is as yet an almost unchartered wilderness, both in the public mind and in that of the sponsors of these bureaus.

III

Older women who have found difficulty in being placed through the agencies or the newspapers will not obtain much relief by turning to the employment managers, especially those of large-scale concerns. Most of the latter are bound, either by the policies of their Board of Directors or through their own initiative, to the policy of hiring younger workers wherever possible. The chief reasons motivating this policy are:

1. The impersonal attitude of business concerns toward their employees, especially if they are a group of smaller firms merged into a larger.

2. The relatively lower cost at which younger workers may be obtained.

3. The fear that older employees, when hired after the thirty or thirty-five year age limit has been passed, may not render service long enough to compensate the firm for possible pensioning.

4. The fact that in New York State all employees working in plants employing four or more operatives, either on or off the premises, come under the Workmen's Compensation Law. This makes it compulsory for firms to insure against possible claims for compensation on the part of employees who meet with accident or illness while at work. Insurance of this nature is usually supplemented by group insurance. The rates for this are higher:

(a) where many women are employed;
(b) in accordance with the rising age of the workers.

These higher insurance rates operate against the employment of older women.

5. Personal preferences, due to the fact that some employers find older women hard to manage. Sometimes the reason is given that young people hold positions of authority over large groups of workers, and do not wish to have older women to whom they would have to give orders.

IV

The State could do much to help simplify the older woman's employment problems:

1. If insurance companies were requested to clarify their reasons for the double rates making it more expensive, first, to hire women at all, and secondly, to hire older women. On the basis of investigations made by the Bureau of Industry of the State, and published by them in a pamphlet entitled "Some Recent Figures on Accidents to Women and Minors" (1926), women are shown to meet with only seven per cent of all the industrial accidents occurring in the State, in spite of the fact that they form a quarter of its working force. Unless these companies can show either that women suffer accident and illness while at work more frequently than do men, or that they are much less regular in attendance, on what basis are these increased rates levied? If it is a question of the expense of the risk involved to the company in writing such insurance, the work of the State Insurance Fund could be extended into these fields

by legislation, since the State Fund need neither make a profit on such insurance, nor need it pay dividends.

2. If the State made the licensing of employment agencies and personnel workers contingent on the passing of examinations to establish their qualifications for carrying on this work.

3. If the State employment agencies now existing were to co-operate more closely with other State bureaus, thus supplementing one another's work. Such co-operation might be gained by a closer affiliation of the State Employment Bureau with the Bureau of Research and the Bureau of Women in Industry.

4. If, in addition, the State were to extend the work of the State Employment Bureau to include one especially organized to aid older workers.

5. If State employment bureaus were to be made at least partially self-supporting. Fees are charged by various State bureaus, such as the Motor License Bureau. Why could not the State agencies charge for their work, if the funds thus acquired were to be used as an aid in obtaining more efficient service both for the employer and for the worker?

6. If legislation were effected compelling employers to give two weeks' notice of intending dismissal to all workers not protected by union membership. This would do away with the pernicious "day to day" contracts now prevailing in some establishments. A more loyal spirit to the firm itself would

inevitably result were the worker made to feel that she was an element in its organization too valuable to be cast aside without consideration.

7. If a State Board of Review were to be established for the hearing of disagreements in the course of which the employee feels that he has been discharged without cause or notification. This would, by the very fact of its existence, do away with many such dismissals. These are sometimes made on the spur of the moment by section heads, upper clerks, floor managers, and other subordinates, who would hesitate to say "You're fired" if they knew they would have to defend such action before a State board. Here, again, industry would gain through the better work done by employees who felt fairly secure about the tenure of their work. If, as no doubt would happen, some employee, taking advantage of the two weeks' notice regulation or of the Review Board regulation, became disagreeable or slackened in her efforts, cause would thereby be established and the employer's action vindicated at the hearing. But such cases would probably happen rarely in comparison with the many that now occur through the abuse of authority on the part of upper subordinates.

Were it felt that a separate Board of Review of this kind might prove too great an expense to the State, the work might be made a part of the duties of the already existing Board of Mediation and Arbitration.

8. If some form of pension were to be sponsored

by the State. This is protection that the worker who has been in the employ of a concern for many years urgently needs. Some firms already have a system of pension protection for such workers, but many more have not. If the State system could be so worked out that the employee herself might contribute the major part of it, in the same way that she might gradually save the total of an endowment life insurance policy, she would probably feel best satisfied in the long run.

9. If there were established a State Loan Fund Bank organized on the general principles governing the Federal Farm Loan Banks. Older women who have the ability to operate a shop but who lack the necessary funds could borrow from this bank for their purpose. Those wishing to draw on it would of course be required to furnish satisfactory references as to character and general ability. One or two of these references might be required to underwrite the loan, so that in case the older woman concerned could not meet her interest payments or liquidate the loan, the fund would not be the loser. The points of advantage of such a bank over privately run loan associations or ordinary bank loans, lie in the long time features and the low interest rates that would form an integral part of the plan, and in the amortization feature that might also form a part of it. Neither the expense nor the possibility of financial loss to the State from the establishment of such a bank would be great compared with the benefits that would be

derived by some older women through its organization.

V

Some older women, by carelessness about personal traits and appearance and by lack of training and application in their youth, have contributed freely to their own work difficulties in middle age. But most older women are normal, well-disposed people, more or less agreeable to get on with, skilled in their vocations through long years of experience in them, fairly intelligent and interested in the important happenings of the day like the rest of humanity. It is these many women who are shut out by arbitrary age barriers. No one expects the unfit to be kept in industry. The superfit will bend some form of industry to their purposes. But the great bulk of older women are adversely affected by these artificial barriers against which they have so far protested in vain.

The social loss from lack of employment for these people is great. The worst feature in it is the throttling of self-respect in the hearts of valuable workers often only because some concerns think that there may be a little more money saved in hiring young workers. By the side of the many constructive measures to build up morale among workers, financed to a considerable extent by wealthy business men, this anomalous treatment of a large segment of working women is so surprising that it can be ascribed only to thoughtlessness or to a lack of understanding of the situation.

Society feels the situation not only in lessened morale for a considerable group, but also in the money loss involved in their incapacity to earn. Their lack of a spending medium permeates all industry. Not only this, but there results a positive expense to the community for medical care and perhaps more, since these women cannot supply their own needs very well when they have no work. If members of their family support them, the financial status of this group is lowered by the amount thus absorbed.

The older woman's position in industry requires much study. The subject is practically an untouched field at present, probably because the older woman's entrance into industry is comparatively recent. Statistics are urgently needed concerning her regularity of attendance when employed, her turnover compared with that of young workers, her average scale of production in the different industries as compared with that of young workers, the wages she receives as compared with these, her points of superiority and her points of inferiority relative to them. Her chief lacks need to be studied and made clear to her, so that she may better understand the nature of the equipment she owes to industry. She cannot charter a career for herself if she be ignorant of the ways of industry in general.

Since the figures regarding payroll and administration matters are confidential with most firms, it would require government sanction to collect enough information about the older woman's share in them to prove of value, and to assure business men that such information would not be misused. Since firms are sure to profit from a study of the situation, they will usually not object to giving information if they can be certain that it will be collected and analyzed by authorities competent to handle it confidentially. There is already established adequate machinery for doing work in this field—in the Women's Bureau of the United States Department of Labor at Washington, D. C., and in the Bureau of Women in Industry of the New York State Department of Labor. There are not many fields into which their researches would prove more interesting to themselves or more profitable to industry and to society as a whole.

VI

In an attempt to summarize the chief angles included in the older woman's present industrial problems, some questions come irresistibly to mind. A few of them follow:

While it is easy to see why young workers may be preferred in many places, why are older women given no opportunity even to apply in some plants? Is the mere fact that a prospective employee is young in itself a guarantee of efficiency, of character, or even of good health? Are not concerns that practise the policy of locking out older women themselves shutting one door through which dependable employees might otherwise enter?

It is sometimes said that older women are captious about the type of work they will accept. Is this exclusively a characteristic of the middle-aged? Is there not rather some ground for assuming that middle-aged women are expected to take anything and be grateful for obtaining it, regardless of their training or preferences? Even if some older women are captious, does that justify any one in looking askance at all older women who want work?

If older women, as some employers assert, are now stagnant and therefore less valuable to them than they think young workers would be, is not that condition to some extent the fault of the plant that employed them? Would it not have been fairer to these workers to have trained them for future progress? Is letting them work as long as the firm felt that they had something to give and then casting them off, altogether just?

Are all older women irritable and inadaptable? Does not an older woman who is lacking in suavity of manner sometimes reflect the general atmosphere of the concern where she is employed? Or may not her attitude conceivably be due to an attempt to fight back a general spirit of dislike directed at her? Are all employers, all upper clerks and managers, always the essence of consideration for their workers? Do they never display the undesirable characteristics for which older women are sometimes denied the chance to support themselves?

Younger people are, as a rule, more agreeable in appearance than older workers. They usually create a less sombre, a more carefree atmosphere in the place where they are congregated than do their older sisters whom experience with life has sobered. Would a proportionate number of older women necessarily wreck the generally cheerful atmosphere? Cannot the labor force be so balanced that workers at both ages may be employed, that each may contribute of what she has most to offer—the younger workers the element of good cheer, the older that of thoroughness?

Where the desire to keep insurance rates down is one of the reasons back of the adverse feeling toward the hiring of older women, how sound is it from a business point of view? One manager who does not hire older women had remarked that business was run for efficiency. When younger saleswomen who are hired to save money, for instance, are unable to handle customers and therefore transact business less profitably than an older and more experienced saleswoman would have done, is this procedure really efficient? Which is greater: the aggregate saving on salaries and insurance rates, or the aggregate loss through fewer and smaller sales? Recalling to mind the figures on rates and salaries previously quoted, is it not rather likely that the loss resulting from a single bungled sale may easily wipe out the saving in rates and salary differences effected over a period of time? In order to obtain the purchaser's point of view, would it not be practicable for shops to send a questionnaire to a carefully selected list of old customers, asking them to evaluate the services of young as against older salespeople in their various departments?

As for the greater pension liability of older women: if pensions become operative only after twenty-five years of service at the minimum, can they be considered as one reason why older women are not desired in some shops? Would an increase in older women mean a very heavily increased drain on the pension system? Some of the employment managers interviewed seemed to feel that a young worker would give much longer service before she became eligible for a pension than an older woman would. That view is understandable when the pension begins only after a certain age has been reached—let us say at the sixty-fifth year. But when it is based on years of service, does it matter at what age work begins, provided that it continue for the twenty-five or thirty-five years necessary before the pension becomes operative?

Sometimes older women are not accorded an opportunity even to interview the employment managers in charge of the plants to which they apply for work. Are they given an even chance when a system of preliminary elimination by an assistant wipes out, as in one instance that was quoted, ninety-five per cent of all applicants before the employment manager even attempts to fill vacancies? Might not the older woman who happens to strike the assistant unfavorably be quite acceptable to the manager himself if she were given an opportunity to face him? Is not the task of giving or denying work to people, on the one hand, and of obtaining the best possible employees for the firm, on the other, vastly important? Is it not so important that only the most expert possible attention—that of the employment manager himself—be given every applicant?

When one considers how different each person is from every other of the same age in general intelligence, background, mental development, experiences in life, difficulties combated, education, personal characteristics, and even general health, how determinative is any fixed age as a standard to be met before an applicant is considered? Is it not true that at twenty-five one woman may be much more run down physically, much less developed mentally, much less reliable than another of the same age? And is it not also true that both may be far less desirable in every valuable business characteristic than another woman of thirty-five or more?

Furthermore, are not most of the employment managers, boards of directors, placement managers in agencies, and single entrepreneurs themselves older than thirty-five—much older, in fact, in many

cases? What would be their feelings were there to
grow up out of some intangible source the idea that
only young people could carry on their work effectively? Suppose the notion were to become current
that only young directors had the vision to see commercial possibilities, and the courage to carry out
their dreams. What if it were to be considered as an
added advantage that a decided saving could be
effected, since young directors could probably be obtained more cheaply? Suppose that older people in
these places were suddenly to be thought too conservative. Suppose that middle-aged employment
managers were to be considered too old-fashioned,
too inadequately trained, for their work. Suppose it
were to be assumed that only young people had the
sympathy necessary for dealing with employees. Suppose it were to be charged that old people in these
places were fussy, cantankerous, unsympathetic, em-
bittered, soured. Suppose it were maintained that
they must be incompetent, since at their age they
were still holding down positions instead of leading
some great commercial enterprise. Suppose it were
found that employment agencies did not function
well enough because so many of the people directing
their policies were middle-aged.

Would not all these people quickly retort that
these notions were unfounded and unjust? Would
they not point to their experience as a valuable asset? Would they not show that it was ridiculous to
judge a man or woman by age figures, since a man

was as old as he felt and a woman as old as she looked? Would they not demonstrate that increasing years bring compensation in the way of growing wisdom, broader sympathies, greater knowledge and consequent power?

Are the industrial and financial losses incident to the pursuance of age barrier policies limited only to the factors immediately affected by them? Can such policies, which close the avenues of self-support to a large and active segment of workers on the one hand, and deprive industry of a large group of efficient workers on the other, long be carried forward without inevitably stamping its effects on the whole structure of industry? Will not all business feel the loss that is bound to ensue when so many workers, because of the erection of age limits, lose their purchasing power? Will not State and charitable institutions feel the strain that must result when many thousands of workers, the majority of whom are able and willing to work, are compelled to come to them for medical and even more fundamental aid? Are not the expenses of these institutions met out of taxes to which all employers, among others, must contribute? Can any employer escape his share?

In a society in which, through centuries of slow development, a sense of social responsibility is just beginning to be aroused—in which this consciousness manifests itself in the building of great housing projects, great hospitals, great research laboratories, great industrial and recreational institutions, and constructive measures of social legislation, all of which are designed primarily to raise the standard of workers as a whole—what defense can be made of policies that block workers from earning the means of self-support after twenty-five, thirty, or thirty-five years of age? Is the fact that large dividends may be declared when lower salaries are paid for younger workers an answer satisfactory to such a society? Is the ideal of such a social group more and more institutions to relieve suffering, or more and more ways to prevent the necessity of establishing institutions to relieve suffering?

Is this attempted scrapping of middle-aged workers in our present stage of industrial development an economic symptom analogous in any way to the scrapping of hand workers in the early days of the Industrial Revolution—a symptom that still manifests itself to-day though in lessened degree whenever new machines change industrial processes? If so, what end is sought by this transition? And what are these many older women expected to do? Are they to go back exclusively to domestic work? Or farm work?

Many more such questions arise. On their wise solution depends the happiness of a great portion of the workers and, through them, of all the social and economic society of which they form so important a part. Since this society is broad enough to embrace us all, and since each of us must face the effects of any social or economic problem that concerns large groups of the whole social unit, can any of us escape either our share of responsibility for trying to answer them or the consequences of society's neglect of them?

CHAPTER II

POSSIBLE FURTHER HELPS TOWARD ITS SOLUTION

I

THE summary of the older woman's industrial problem that has just been concluded outlines the elements she herself has contributed to it, and those for which the employer is chiefly responsible. Some of the lines along which the State and Society in general are affected, and some of the ways in which these might aid in the problem's solution have been indicated. The older woman's educational background, too, has been considered as a factor that has undoubtedly added some weight to its complexities. It now remains to indicate a few of the ways in which foresight and the improvement of existing machinery may aid in stemming its future aggravation and complication. For it is now generally recognized that the best way to cure an adverse situation is to prevent its development.

Both employers and older people frequently put the blame for the latter's present unfavorable economic condition on the fact that they did not plan ahead far enough in the beginning of their industrial careers. As they look back into the years of their youth, the realization comes to many that close application in evening courses giving advanced training in their fields might have made them more valuable and more desirable to employers. They see now that evenings spent in this way instead of following the will-o-the-wisp of "O-well-we're-young-only-once" might have returned high interest on the investment of some of their leisure time.

Yet, even if through lack of foresight they are now less favorably situated than they might have been, older women need not therefore sit back in resigned despair. The following paragraphs are reprinted from a recent brief article in the New York *Sunday World Magazine** quoting statements concerning experiments by Dr. E. L. Thorndike of Columbia University:

"A person under fifty years of age should be encouraged to learn anything new that he wants to and should not hesitate for fear of being too old to learn. To a lesser degree this is also true for the man or woman over fifty years.

"In Dr. Thorndike's experiments the learning abilities of a group of average age twenty-two years was compared with one of average age of forty-two years. The older group learned about five-sixths as fast as the younger but both learned more quickly than children. Apparently learning ability rises to the age of twenty years, then after a stationary period of some years declines very slowly.

* October 12, 1927.

"It is not age or lack of ability that keeps adults from learning a new language or trade but lack of opportunity or desire."

She may, therefore, still better her condition, whatever may have caused her past indifference to self-improvement. Even though it may prove a long, rough climb over the mountain of accumulated inertia to the top of specialized proficiency, it can be accomplished, especially if the road chosen for reaching the summit goes over fields of work for which the older woman has a distinct liking.

That such effort does lead to success is shown in the following quotations from a letter appearing in the New York *Times* of October 17, 1927:

"Stricken with a serious illness at past fifty years and having spent practically all his savings in medical and family expenses during convalescent unemployment, a friend of mine in the last two years has risen to the top of his trade. Although he may never regain his health, employers began making rival offers for his services as soon as they learned that he could work. They knew well that during a quarter century of experience he had developed a technical skill and knowledge which they could not easily find elsewhere.

"An aspect this of the middle-aged unemployment problem which has not, I think, been sufficiently brought out.

"There is a best way even to dig a trench, to add a column, to sell a shoelace, to word a phrase; and the man who in early life forces himself to learn and practice permanently this technical excellence need never fear a middle age, or even an old age, of unemployment."

Thus, whatever may have brought about the erstwhile incomplete training of the older woman, there seems to be little justification for its continuance. Assuming that she is anxious now to develop her capacities as fully as possible, what opportunities are open to her?

First, there are the evening schools. If her elementary school training has been adequate, the high schools will give her more aid than those of lower grade. Courses in salesmanship, in business English, in secretarial work, in economics, in business organization, in commercial law, in accounting, and in foreign languages are at her command free of charge. Out of the wide range offered by the present-day free evening high schools she may choose much that, if conscientiously followed, must make her a more valuable employee to any concern.

Such courses will open to her avenues of further usefulness, will kindle her mentally, will make her comprehension of the aims and scope of industry as a whole much clearer. They will add to her machine-like perfection of technic the touch that is needed to lift her out of the ranks of the mechanical routine workers into the group of those whose efforts are guided by intelligent understanding of the relation of their work to that of the rest of the concern. The changed angle of approach to her work, which is bound to result from her increased training, cannot fail to make of her a more effective worker. Should the age limitation policy operate against present workers as it now operates against new applicants, these better-trained workers would, because of their increased value to their firms, be in a much stronger position to be retained than would those who had done nothing to improve their equipment.

Older women who have already developed themselves along the lines suggested would probably find courses in literature, art appreciation, and music stimulating. Work in the study of the drama, based on visits to current productions, often prove most interesting, not only because of the attractiveness of the material itself, but also on account of the brisk class discussions that usually follow the witnessing of any absorbing dramatic work. Studies in social subjects, in politics and government, in history, in science, are available to those whose interests lie in these directions. Those who like to make things with their hands will find instruction ready for them in millinery and dressmaking. In this age of high educational requirements in industry the older woman who does not make use of her opportunities to take up some work that will advance her mental growth is allowing herself to be less efficient than her employer has a right, under the circumstances, to expect her to be.

Nor may inexperienced women expect to enter industry without offering some definite service to it. If she has household experience, that is what she has to sell. The New York *Sun* of February 4, 1928, gives an account, for instance, of the activities of one woman who turned her knowledge of household management to good account by establishing a school for the training of brides and their would-be maids.

"I have been successful," says this woman, "simply because I used such knowledge as all successful housewives have, and because I wanted to supply the needs of other women—particularly those which other people had overlooked. There is an endless field for women along these lines, if they are not afraid to launch an original project."

If the woman untrained in the ways of industry does not wish to utilize her knowledge of housekeeping, industry will expect her to take the trouble to learn something else. Even then she must realize that the technical knowledge thus gained will need to be supplemented by some experience before she can hope to be a really valuable worker. She offers something to sell. Industry is her customer. It will not buy a product that has not been carefully planned with any greater degree of avidity than she herself would display in (let us say) purchasing in a shop a dress made by an amateur.

II

As has been stated, the best way to cure an adverse situation is to prevent its development. That holds quite as true for the young worker as for the older woman.

The careless, indifferent, thoughtless, poorly

equipped young worker of to-day becomes the older-woman problem of to-morrow. Youth has a way of slipping past before we know it, and age barriers now appear to be slipping ever backward to meet the vanishing years of first youth. Before the young routine worker realizes it, she will have come to the twenty-five-year bar.

What will she do thereafter? The answer to that question depends largely on her foresight. If she has studied modern industrial conditions and modern employment tendencies she will be fully aware of the quicksands which, as an older routine worker, appear under present conditions to yawn for her. She will therefore give serious thought to their avoidance. She will obtain the fullest training and the most complete mastery of her special field that she can possibly grasp. She will realize the importance of a desirable personality to her progress. She will try if possible to develop herself in some field where she may be comparatively independent. Highly specialized training of a type certain to be well in demand, or the opening of a business of her own, appear at present to be her means to that end.

Expert educational procedure could do much to help her to a greater extent than is now the case even with our present improved facilities, for educational systems, like all other living organisms, must keep on growing and developing. There is need at present for more trade schools and more vocational schools, as well as for more diversified courses in the already established schools. These would help to salvage the many young people who, in spite of all that is done, still go out into industry without definite or adequate preparation, because nothing that we have at present quite fits their requirements. There is need, too, for more study and development in the field of vocational guidance. These added improvements will not make executives out of young people whose natural aptitudes fit them rather for routine work; but it will make of them routine people skilled in the fields best suited to their capabilities, with minds open to future possibilities for themselves if they are strong enough to take advantage of them. But, above all, there is need to emphasize in these schools the unfortunate position of the present-day routine worker in industry who has neglected to make the fullest possible use of her opportunities.

This educational campaign could be extended beyond the schools so as to reach the general public. Were it to be made comprehensive, older workers now handicapped by poor training or irritating personalities might be inspired to eradicate these failings. Employers might come to see that a blanket barrier that shuts out the comparatively few undesirable older women keeps out also many well qualified workers. Many unjust conditions that tend to make the older woman's position less secure—such as day to day contracts in shops, placement clerks not always expert enough for their work, and the lack of a pension system in some establishments—would come under the searchlight of public opinion. The far reaching economic effects of such policies throughout the fabric of industry would be recognized.

The acquisition of a more thorough education, then, both general and specifically applied to intensive work in her own field, is one way in which the older woman may make her position more secure, and the young worker make hers less liable to loss in later years. The advantages of this fuller training are in New York City open to them for the asking.

III

Let us assume that the older woman, on her part, has done all she can to make herself more desirable industrially by improving her general education and her technical equipment. Let us suppose that she has come to realize that a neat appearance and a pleasant manner are good letters of introduction, and that a business office that does not wish to accept the methods imported from her last position has the inalienable right to prefer its own. Let us take for granted that she does not object to travelling to and from work; that she is willing to accept work with firms situated in undesirable neighborhoods; that she will accept a low salary to begin, even in cases where she has formerly held a fairly remunerative post; that she is resigned to employment that compels working very early in the morning or very late in the evening—that, in brief, she is ready to take any legitimate position that may be offered her. What additional co-operation, beyond what is already at her command, may be given her by the chief mediums for finding her employment—the newspaper advertisements and the employment agencies?

Let us consider the newspaper advertisements first. They attempt to facilitate her search by classifying her needs and her capabilities into groups. But they would no doubt prove a still more effective medium if both the "Situations Wanted" and the "Help Wanted" sections were to be classified into groupings narrower than they are at present. *The Times* does something of this when it places into one division all advertisements inserted by employment agencies, which in *The World* are scattered promiscuously through the "Want" columns.

Older women would find their search facilitated if all the positions calling for canvassing in any form were to be put into one division openly and honestly labelled, no matter under what masquerade they might present themselves for insertion. Also clerical work, the sewing occupations, and selling in shops might each have its own division.

But the section most in need of revision is the one called "Household," whether it be for "Help Wanted" or for "Situations Wanted." Into this division are now jumbled all types of employment and of workers. The only connecting link among them, apparently, is the fact that somehow or somewhere they all relate to work done in the home rather than in shop or factory. We find in this one group appeals for and applications from dressmakers, governesses, trained nurses, and companion-secretaries. Would not a group labelled "Domestic Service" divide the kind of work commonly indicated by the term "household duties" from those other fields? This would avoid confusion and irritation for both employer and worker.

A further refinement of the suggested "Domestic Service" columns into groups of houseworkers, on the basis of their willingness to work for one, two, four, six, or more persons, would be a valuable aid at least to the employer. But that is perhaps too much to ask.

IV

What can the employment agencies still do to aid the older woman in finding work? For one thing, if the contact man or woman in privately run agencies, who is really the sales agent for the bureau's services, would make it a point to feature the older women registrants, and to call attention to their desirable qualities, it might materially help to increase the older woman's opportunities. It is particularly surprising that they do not do so to any great extent, in view of the fact that most of the contact people, as well as most of the placement clerks and managers in these offices, are themselves middle-aged. This is also true of those women who operate their own agencies.

Both large and small agencies, as has before been indicated, deny that it is their policy to refrain from sending out older women applicants in answer to calls. They go further, and express the deepest sympathy with the middle-aged woman and her problems. But they declare themselves helpless to combat a situation that they did not create. It is here that they are in error. They could do much, as has already been suggested; for most employers want, first and foremost, the best services they can obtain for the salaries they will pay. If they can only be convinced that youth is in itself no more a guarantee of satisfactory service than middle age is necessarily a bar to it, a long step in the adjustment of employment difficulties will have been taken.

Then again, both large and small agencies could help older women in another way were they sincerely disposed to do so. Incidentally new fields for older women would be opened up with its adoption. Every office receives calls from older women whose general appearance and manner are in themselves obstacles in their search for work. It is suggested that each employment office have on its staff a "personality adviser" whose duty it would be to confer with each applicant in regard to these gaps in her commercial qualifications. This adviser would have to be an older woman of infinite tact, real sympathy, and personal charm, to do her difficult work effectively and yet without offense. So often the defects that stand in the way of older women might be eradicated were they but made conscious of them. This is a long, hard step away from the present method of merely registering older women, deciding mentally that they will not do, and, then wearing them out by the discouraging "nothing to-day," repeated until the applicant finally tires of calling at that particular agency. But such a step would bring the agency's efforts much nearer to the important factor it might be in the making of worth-while industrial adjustments. It is far beyond the merely haphazard supplying of employees and places that is now often all that agencies attempt.

Many of those who now do only the most rudimentary details of placement work could, under such a system, devote themselves entirely to the work of taking down the names and addresses on both sides of the transaction, and other such routine work, leaving the actual placement to experts. If these were older women with much the same personal qualifications as those suggested for the "personnel doctor," many industrial misfits and consequent all-around losses would inevitably be averted. After a time really sincere work along these lines would result in fewer turnovers, in less tragedy among the middle-aged, and in the elimination of artificial restrictions, such as age barriers, that now hamper fluidity in the labor market.

But, one asks, would such changed conditions not necessarily bring about the ruin of the employment agency business through decreasing the number of applicants that come to them for places, or reducing the number of positions? On the contrary; for three influences would operate to correct any such possible tendency. First, some older women would immediately be absorbed in filling the two types of positions outlined. That would release their old places to newcomers. Secondly, industry normally keeps expanding with new wants and new inventions. It therefore automatically requires an ever-increasing labor force to carry on its work. Thirdly, every older woman who finds work directly helps industrial growth. These women are customers as well as workers. When they do not earn, they cannot spend. But when they do earn, business is increased by their demand for the goods and services they buy with their earnings. This aids business expansion; and consequently there is need of more new workers.

Not only could the private agencies thus extend their work, but the public agencies, too, could still do much more. Surely if improvement in employment agency administration for the older woman is to begin anywhere, it is here, where the office is run by the public for its citizens, purely as a civic function and not to make money. It is here that the employment problem could be studied as a social and not as a routine question. Contacts could be made on behalf of middle-aged workers under the auspices of the State that for many reasons would be beyond the reach of employment agencies run primarily as business enterprises.

Some possibilities for bringing about better results for the older woman suggest themselves. Public-spirited, sympathetic, well educated women could be given charge of the contact branch of the service. The interviewing and the placement, too, could be covered by older women interested in the work, capable of winning the confidence of the applicants, and able to direct them into the fields best suited to their various capacities. But the greatest service that well qualified placement managers could render these applicants comes in helping these older women to retain their self-respect intact, unbruised by that feeling of uselessness so often the result of their unsuccessful encounters in private agencies. The spirit of the public agency could be such as to engender in the applicant the conviction that she had her value to the community as a member thereof, and that the community, on its part, realized this and would do all it could to put her where she could contribute it.

A bureau so organized could embark on an extensive advertising campaign. Firms and employees who had tested its value would help materially to make it still better known. A scientifically run public bureau once firmly established, improvement in the administration of privately run agencies would have to follow as a matter of self-preservation. They would have to be continually on the alert to meet the standard set by the model agency operated by the State, well knowing that if they could not reach it loss of business would result. And all industry would benefit by this advance in running employment agencies.

V

At present the older woman is more or less passive and helpless in the face of conditions that threaten her very means of livelihood. She is passive because singly she can do little to combat the situation. Would some form of organization, such as labor organization for women in the white collar occupations, help her?

Such labor unions could admit both young and older women. These organizations could let it be understood that they would not champion the cause of an older woman or admit her to membership if she possessed no other qualification than that of her age. They could demand a rigorous standard of attainment both in achievement and in personality. They could pledge to employers the upholding of those standards. They could plan and execute educational campaigns for the mental and the technical improvement of all their workers, both young and middle-aged.

On the other hand such organizations have many faults. They are inclined to narrow rigidly the limits within which certain employees may work. They ought, because of their affiliation of many trades and industries into a great federation, to be able to shift workers from quiet to busy related industries between seasons; but they are not much inclined to help labor fluidity. The white collar occupations, because in some cases the number of workers of this type in any one plant is comparatively limited, would require a type of organization very difficult to handle and to administer. The peculiar personal relations between employers and employees in these occupations make the successful interpolation of group bargaining a matter of delicate adjustment.

Yet if out of the organization of the white collar workers better conditions for the older woman would result, the employer, too, would gain in the long run, and with him all industry. For bad economic conditions in any one labor group inevitably affect the whole economic fabric, and their improvement, on the other hand, must benefit all industry.

VI

What, if anything, can be done to shift workers from complex to less difficult positions as they advance in years? Where the work is quite elementary in character, and where the question involved is mainly one of lessening its physical strain as the workers grow older, the task of shifting them from more strenuous to lighter tasks is a comparatively easy one. Factory operatives can readily enough be transferred from machines that require rapid movements and strained attention to those easier to tend, or to putting the final touches on the finished product that can best be done by hand. Certain branches of an industry, such as hand finishing in the cloth dress factories and the same work in silk dress factories, might be dovetailed so that the alternating seasons for these commodities could be made the means of using one shift of older workers continually for both types of factories. Such dovetailing could be inaugurated in other seasonal trades where the painstaking handwork of older women would be an asset.

It is in the more highly trained and specialized fields that it becomes increasingly difficult to shift aging workers. Elderly salespeople might perhaps be given work requiring shorter hours, or part time work. In large scale concerns elderly clerical workers might probably be found useful in caring for office supplies and in taking personal charge of existing office equipment. Especially well qualified elderly women might fill a long-felt need in some of these concerns as advisers-at-large to beginners.

But in general the attempt to articulate more complex with easier work as the employee grows older meets with complications that vary upward with the previously attained skill of the worker to be shifted. Personal elements step in to make the situation more and more difficult of adjustment. Unless work equally responsible could be found for the elderly woman deposed from a good position because of her age, the blow to her pride inflicted by the transfer would be none the easier to overcome because her lessened capacity for work made necessary this concession to her age. Partly because of this fact and partly because some degree of readjustment to her new position would be necessary, her services to the industry that tried the experiment might not prove as valuable, perhaps, as those she would have rendered to it had she retained her old place.

In view of these things it is doubtful whether either industry or the elderly workers themselves would derive much benefit from such employment shifts. It would appear that a sound plan of annuity for the worker, to be hers after a certain number of years of service had been completed, and to which she herself had contributed at least some portion, would prove not only a better solution for the worker, but also a much fairer one for the employer. For the latter would not then have as active workers on his force those who could no longer lend their best efforts to it. Nor would the former need to accept a post less important and dignified than that which she had previously held. The worker could retire with the memory of work fully done as long as the position she held was in her care; and the employer too would retain that impression of her services.

VII

If, then, side by side with an open-minded attitude toward older women on the part of employers, on the one hand, and State aid to relieve some of the simpler yet far-reaching elements in the problem, on the other, older women would, on their part, take under serious consideration the elimination of such elements in their personal appearance and attitude as might so far have been found undesirable by employers, the most pressing immediate factors in the older woman's industrial problem would find fairly prompt relief. The worst features of wide-spread unemployment for her would be stemmed. In the meantime, through earnest study of her needs and her capabilities on the part of government bureaus, not only she but also the general public would become aware of her industrial possibilities and handicaps. She may need to begin now a course of training that would make her more valuable to business, so that she herself may prove an aid to the solution of her own problem. The prevention of serious future augmentation of the ranks of untrained older workers through the careful development of our present-day young people may well be recognized as a powerful factor in hemming its further growth. The gradual building up of the public and private employment agencies into specialized bureaus for really intelligent labor placements, and the strengthening of the classified advertisement columns of the newspapers, would help in the future rounding out of the problem's sharpest angles. The organization of women in the white collar trades into unions might prove an aid to them in establishing for themselves more favorable conditions, especially in regard to tenure of position; and might help employers through the establishment of standards to which older women who wished to retain their positions must conform. Mutual understanding of each other's side is necessary—by industry, that the older woman's position and possible contributions to business may properly be evaluated; by the older woman, that her responsibilities to the industrial system of which she forms a part may duly be recognized.

Changing times and conditions have turned from the home into industry a new figure—the middle-aged woman. She looms larger and ever larger in the business field. With her entrance into the field of industry have come problems that concern her particularly. They must be solved—for she has entered industrial life to stay.

What solutions will be found for them? That remains for the employer, for the agencies, for her, for society, all acting in co-operation, to discover and to decide.

PUBLICATIONS CONSULTED

American Labor Legislative Review; Dec., 1927.
  Commercial Insurance *vs.* State Funds.
  Old Age Pension Legislation.
Brissenden, P. L., and Frankel, E.
  Labor Turnover in Industry, 1922.
Brissenden, P. L. Monthly Labor Review, Apr., 1927.
  Bibliography of Labor Turnover.
Equitable Life Assurance Society.
  General Summary of Group Insurance Rules and
    Procedure.
  Suggestions for Selling Group Insurance.
Fourteenth Federal Census, Vol. 9, Occupations, 1920.
New York *Sunday Times,* The; July–Nov. inclusive, 1927.
New York *Sunday World,* The; July–Nov. inclusive, 1927.
Publications of the Women's Bureau, U. S. Dept. of Labor.
  Facts About Working Women. 1920.
  Report of the Director, 1925, 1926.
  Short Talks About Working Women. 1927.
Publications of the Dept. of Labor, State of New York;
  Division of Women in Industry.
  Women Who Work. 1922.
  Hours and Earnings of Women in Five Industries.
    1923.
  Some Recent Figures on Accidents to Women and
    Minors. 1926.
Turnover of Labor, The; Federal Board for Vocational
  Education; Washington, D. C.
Wilson, I. M. Industrial Management, Jan., 1919.
  Women Workers and Turnover.
Workmen's Compensation Law for New York State;
  Amended to Aug. 1, 1927.

INDEX

INDEX

Women in America

FROM COLONIAL TIMES TO THE 20TH CENTURY

An Arno Press Collection

Andrews, John B. and W. D. P. Bliss. **History of Women in Trade Unions** (*Report on Conditions of Woman and Child Wage-Earners in the United States,* Vol. X; 61st Congress, 2nd Session, Senate Document No. 645). 1911

Anthony, Susan B. **An Account of the Proceedings on the Trial of Susan B. Anthony, on the Charge of Illegal Voting at the Presidential Election in November, 1872,** and on the Trial of Beverly W. Jones, Edwin T. Marsh and William B. Hall, the Inspectors of Election by Whom her Vote was Received. 1874

The Autobiography of a Happy Woman. 1915

Ayer, Harriet Hubbard. **Harriet Hubbard Ayer's Book:** A Complete and Authentic Treatise on the Laws of Health and Beauty. 1902

Barrett, Kate Waller. **Some Practical Suggestions on the Conduct of a Rescue Home.** *Including* **Life of Dr. Kate Waller Barrett** (Reprinted from *Fifty Years' Work With Girls* by Otto Wilson). [1903]

Bates, Mrs. D. B. **Incidents on Land and Water;** Or, Four Years on the Pacific Coast. 1858

Blumenthal, Walter Hart. **Women Camp Followers of the American Revolution.** 1952

Boothe, Viva B., editor. **Women in the Modern World** (*The Annals of the American Academy of Political and Social Science,* Vol. CXLIII, May 1929). 1929

Bowne, Eliza Southgate. **A Girl's Life Eighty Years Ago:** Selections from the Letters of Eliza Southgate Bowne. 1888

Brooks, Geraldine. **Dames and Daughters of Colonial Days.** 1900

Carola Woerishoffer: Her Life and Work. 1912

Clement, J[esse], editor. **Noble Deeds of American Women;** With Biographical Sketches of Some of the More Prominent. 1851

Crow, Martha Foote. **The American Country Girl.** 1915

De Leon, T[homas] C. **Belles, Beaux and Brains of the 60's.**
1909

de Wolfe, Elsie (Lady Mendl). **After All.** 1935

Dix, Dorothy (Elizabeth Meriwether Gilmer). **How to Win and
Hold a Husband.** 1939

Donovan, Frances R. **The Saleslady.** 1929

Donovan, Frances R. **The Schoolma'am.** 1938

Donovan, Frances R. **The Woman Who Waits.** 1920

Eagle, Mary Kavanaugh Oldham, editor. **The Congress of
Women,** Held in the Woman's Building, World's Columbian
Exposition, Chicago, U.S.A., 1893. 1894

Ellet, Elizabeth F. **The Eminent and Heroic Women of America.**
1873

Ellis, Anne. **The Life of an Ordinary Woman.** 1929

[Farrar, Eliza W. R.] **The Young Lady's Friend.** By a Lady.
1836

Filene, Catherine, editor. **Careers for Women.** 1920

Finley, Ruth E. **The Lady of Godey's:** Sarah Josepha Hale. 1931
Fragments of Autobiography. 1974

Frost, John. **Pioneer Mothers of the West;** Or, Daring and
Heroic Deeds of American Women. 1869

[Gilman], Charlotte Perkins Stetson. **In This Our World.** 1899

Goldberg, Jacob A. and Rosamond W. Goldberg. **Girls on the
City Streets:** A Study of 1400 Cases of Rape. 1935

Grace H. Dodge: Her Life and Work. 1974

Greenbie, Marjorie Barstow. **My Dear Lady:** The Story of Anna
Ella Carroll, the "Great Unrecognized Member of Lincoln's
Cabinet." 1940

Hourwich, Andria Taylor and Gladys L. Palmer, editors. **I Am
a Woman Worker:** A Scrapbook of Autobiographies. 1936

Howe, M[ark] A. De Wolfe. **Memories of a Hostess:**
A Chronicle of Friendships Drawn Chiefly from the Diaries of
Mrs. James T. Fields. 1922

Irwin, Inez Haynes. **Angels and Amazons:** A Hundred Years of
American Women. 1934

Laughlin, Clara E. **The Work-a-Day Girl:** A Study of Some Present-Day Conditions. 1913

Lewis, Dio. **Our Girls.** 1871

Liberating the Home. 1974

Livermore, Mary A. **The Story of My Life; Or,** The Sunshine and Shadow of Seventy Years . . . To Which is Added Six of Her Most Popular Lectures. 1899

Lives to Remember. 1974

Lobsenz, Johanna. **The Older Woman in Industry.** 1929

MacLean, Annie Marion. **Wage-Earning Women.** 1910

Meginness, John F. **Biography of Frances Slocum, the Lost Sister of Wyoming:** A Complete Narrative of her Captivity of Wanderings Among the Indians. 1891

Nathan, Maud. **Once Upon a Time and Today.** 1933

[Packard, Elizabeth Parsons Ware]. **Great Disclosure of Spiritual Wickedness!!** In High Places. With an Appeal to the Government to Protect the Inalienable Rights of Married Women. 1865

Parsons, Alice Beal. **Woman's Dilemma.** 1926

Parton, James, et al. **Eminent Women of the Age:** Being Narratives of the Lives and Deeds of the Most Prominent Women of the Present Generation. 1869

Paton, Lucy Allen. **Elizabeth Cary Agassiz:** A Biography. 1919

Rayne, M[artha] L[ouise]. **What Can a Woman Do;** Or, Her Position in the Business and Literary World. 1893

Richmond, Mary E. and Fred S. Hall. **A Study of Nine Hundred and Eighty-Five Widows Known to Certain Charity Organization Societies in 1910.** 1913

Ross, Ishbel. **Ladies of the Press:** The Story of Women in Journalism by an Insider. 1936

Sex and Equality. 1974

Snyder, Charles McCool. **Dr. Mary Walker:** The Little Lady in Pants. 1962

Stow, Mrs. J. W. **Probate Confiscation:** Unjust Laws Which Govern Woman. 1878

Sumner, Helen L. **History of Women in Industry in the United**

States (*Report on Conditions of Woman and Child Wage-Earners in the United States,* Vol. IX; 61st Congress, 2nd Session, Senate Document No. 645). 1910

[Vorse, Mary H.] **Autobiography of an Elderly Woman.** 1911

Washburn, Charles. **Come into My Parlor:** A Biography of the Aristocratic Everleigh Sisters of Chicago. 1936

Women of Lowell. 1974

Woolson, Abba Gould. **Dress-Reform:** A Series of Lectures Delivered in Boston on Dress as it Affects the Health of Women. 1874

Working Girls of Cincinnati. 1974